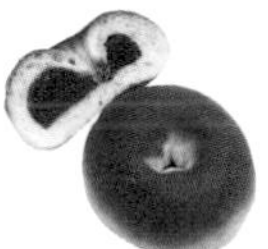

Explanatory notes
凡例

ⓘTelephone number 電話番号
ⒶAddress 住所
ⓄBusiness hours 営業時間
ⒸRegular holiday 定休日
ⒻFee 料金

TOKYO NOW

巨大観光都市・東京の今

Tokyo Station

Tokyo the capital — growing to become the center of Japan over nearly 400 years since the Edo period (1603-1867). It is one of the largest cities in the world in terms of population and economy. Just a stroll around Tokyo will bring you to the leading edge of the world's fashion, whilst you will encounter the many reminiscences of the good old Japanese culture inherited in daily life... The urban scene of Tokyo, where the new and the old come together, is what makes the capital fascinating and different from elsewhere.

There are currently two areas worth a visit and they are Roppongi and around Tokyo station. In recent years many large complexes have been completed in these areas, such as Roppongi Hills and Tokyo Midtown in the former, also Daimaru department store and Shin-Marunouchi Building in the latter. These areas have now become great touristic spots that accommodate large numbers of attractive shops and restaurants. The two facilities in Roppongi in particular include an art museum within the complex and have contributed to making Roppongi the Art Town together with The National Art Center, Tokyo, whose impressive architecture was designed by the late Kisho Kurokawa and opened in 2007. Meanwhile, the front entrance to Tokyo — Tokyo station and its surroundings — are currently undergoing redevelopment. The classic red-brick station building and the high-rise buildings that glance down at the spread of green canopy in the Imperial Palace that faces the station have now become a representative scene of Tokyo.

The National Art Center Tokyo (P21)

江戸時代（1603〜1867）より約400年に渡って日本の中心として発展し続ける、首都・東京。人口、経済規模ともに世界最大の都市の一つである。街を歩くだけで世界の流行の最先端を呼吸できると同時に、暮らしの中で綿々と受け継がれてきた古きよき日本文化の面影がそこここに残る…。新旧混然一体となった都市風景が、ほかのどことも違う東京の魅力と言えるだろう。

今、観光的に注目のエリアは二つ、六本木と東京駅周辺。前者は「六本木ヒルズ」、「東京ミッドタウン」後者は「新丸ビル」に百貨店の「大丸」と、近年相次いで大型複合施設が完成。レストランやショップなど、話題を集める店が数多く入る一大観光スポットになった。特に六本木の2施設は共に美術館を併設し、同じく2007年に開館した、黒川紀章氏の設計によるフォルムも印象的な「国立新美術館」と合わせて“アートの街、六本木”の顔に。東京の表玄関となる東京駅とその周辺は、目下再開発の只中。レトロな赤レンガの駅舎と、駅正面に広がる皇居の深い緑を見下ろす高層ビル群は、東京の今を象徴する風景といえる。

TOKYO
The Greatest Travel Tips

英語で歩く東京

SIGHTSEEING
EATING&DRINKING
SHOPPING
LEISURE
STAY
WORDBOOK

Contents

Tokyo Midtown (P20)

Komakata dojo (P14)

In addition to these areas is the shitamachi area visited also by many foreign tourists who come to discover the traditional Nippon, where retrospective shopping malls, town houses, craftsmen streets and temples still remain. Besides the ever-popular Asakusa areas like Yanaka and Nezu have also attracted attention in recent years. Meanwhile, Akihabara, the Mecca of the 'otaku' movement originally famed for its status as home appliances town, is yet another popular area that attracts many foreign tourists.

When it comes to shopping it has to be Ginza and Omotesando. These areas are home to a line of flagship shops of world's top brands, with constant appearances of new shops. Some sidewalk brand boutiques even include a café or restaurant as part of their brand designing, shaping these towns into classy zones fit for the sophisticated adults. On the other hand, one must not forget also Harajuku and Shibuya, the Mecca areas for young people's fashion where internationally popular street brands such as BAPE® and NEIGHBORHOOD were born.

With eight Japanese and Western-style restaurants acquiring the 3-stars status in the Michelin Guide, Tokyo's culinary offering is getting a new world recognition for its capabilities. One could say that Tokyo is now a place with the most diverse offering of cuisines in the world. While we see top restaurants with internationally acclaimed star chefs opening one after another, fast food shops offering original Japanese foods like ramen and gyudon are also in for the fierce competition. You should try traditional tastes such as sukiyaki with Japan's own brand beef, or tempura using ingredients à la Tokyo.

Asakusa Imahan (P52)

一方、昔ながらの商店街や町屋、職人町、寺院などが残り、"ニッポン"の原風景を訪ねて海外からも多くの観光客が訪れるのが下町エリア。不動の人気の浅草をはじめ、近年は谷中・根津などが注目を集めている。元々は家電の街として有名であったが、"オタク"ムーブメントの聖地となった秋葉原も、外国人観光客が多く集まる人気エリアだ。

ショッピングと言えば、銀座に表参道。世界の一流ブランドの旗艦店が並び、新規の出店も続々。カフェやレストランなどを併設するものもあり、各ブランドの意匠を凝らした路面店が、大人が似合うハイソな町並みを形づくっている。また、若者ファッションのメッカで、BAPE®やNEIGHBORHOODなど、世界的に人気のストリート系ブランド誕生の地でもある原宿、渋谷も外せない。

2007年、ミシュランのレストランガイドで和洋ジャンルも様々な8軒が3つ星を獲得し、改めてその実力を世界に知らしめたのが東京の食。今や、世界で最も多種多様な料理が食べられる町、と言っていいだろう。海外のスターシェフの名を冠した高級店が続々出店する一方、"ラーメン"や"牛丼"など、日本独特のファストフード店もしのぎを削る。国産ブランド牛を使用したすき焼きや、江戸前の素材を使用した天ぷらなどの伝統の味も一度は味わってみたい。

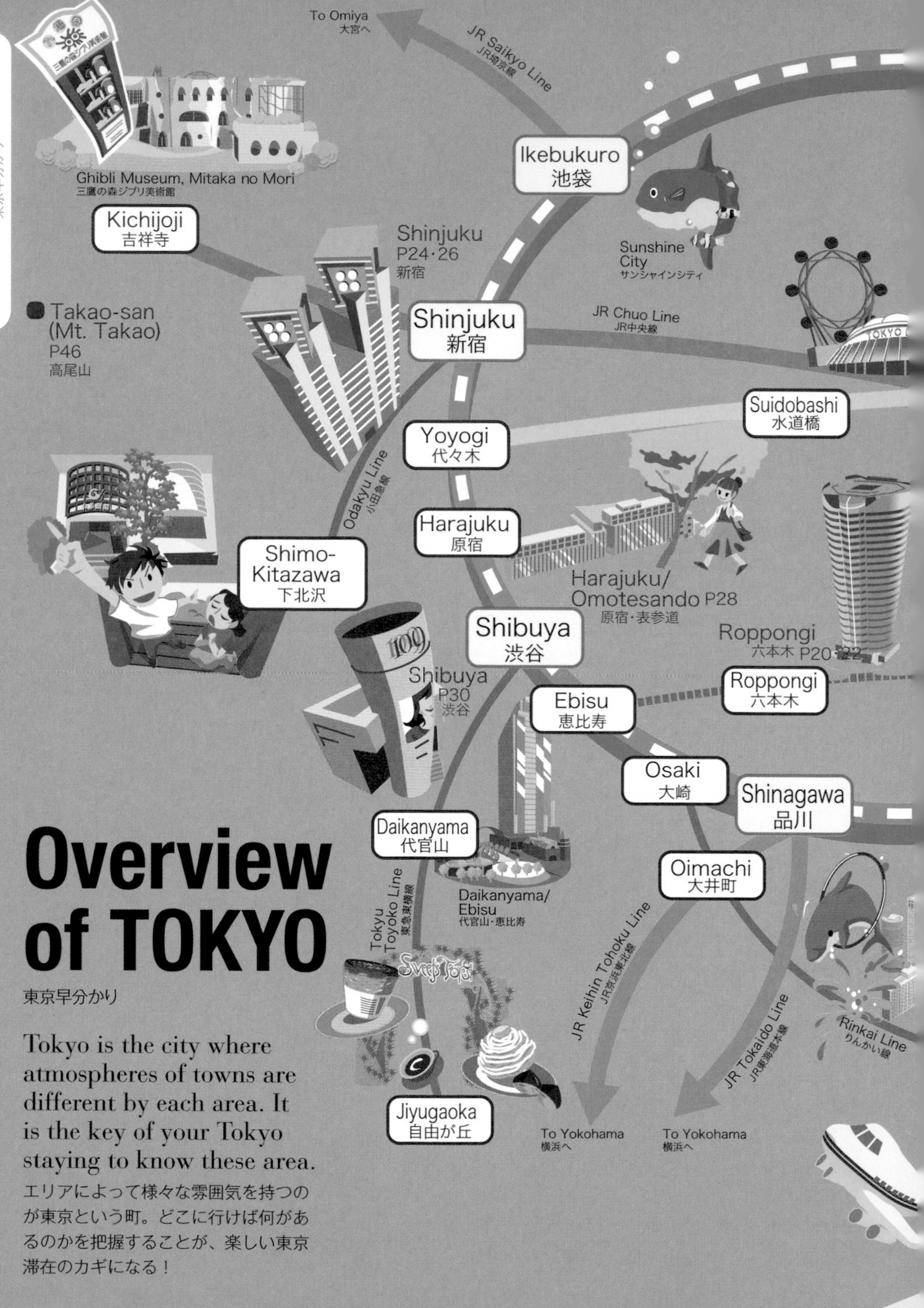

Overview of TOKYO

東京早分かり

Tokyo is the city where atmospheres of towns are different by each area. It is the key of your Tokyo staying to know these area.

エリアによって様々な雰囲気を持つのが東京という町。どこに行けば何があるのかを把握することが、楽しい東京滞在のカギになる！

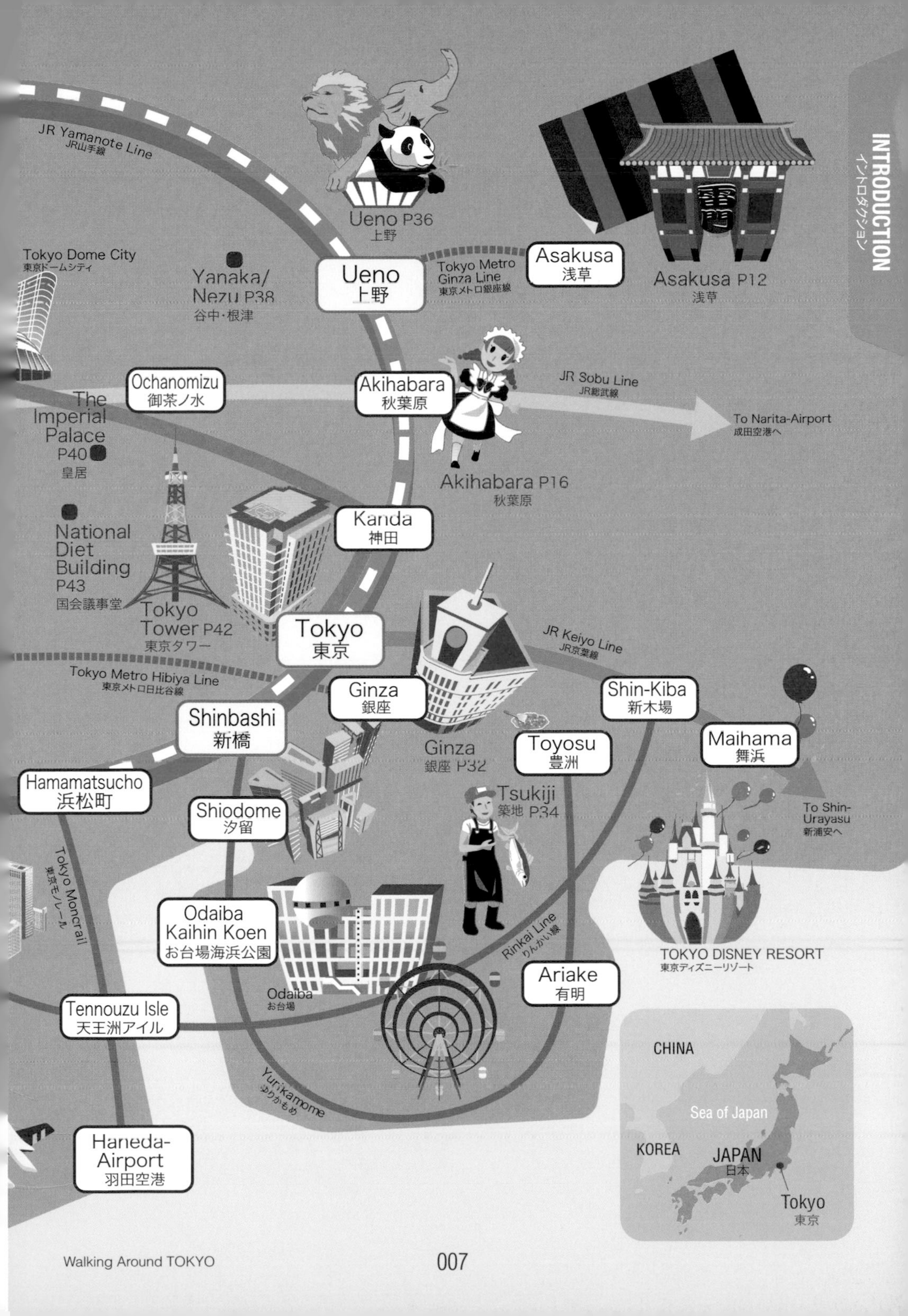

INTRODUCTION
イントロダクション
JR Yamanote Line
JR山手線
Ueno P36
上野
Tokyo Dome City
東京ドームシティ
Yanaka/
Nezu P38
谷中・根津
Ueno
上野
Tokyo Metro
Ginza Line
東京メトロ銀座線
Asakusa
浅草
Asakusa P12
浅草
Ochanomizu
御茶ノ水
The
Imperial
Palace
P40
皇居
Akihabara
秋葉原
JR Sobu Line
JR総武線
To Narita-Airport
成田空港へ
Akihabara P16
秋葉原
National
Diet
Building
P43
国会議事堂
Kanda
神田
Tokyo
Tower P42
東京タワー
Tokyo
東京
JR Keiyo Line
JR京葉線
Tokyo Metro Hibiya Line
東京メトロ日比谷線
Ginza
銀座
Shin-Kiba
新木場
Shinbashi
新橋
Ginza
銀座 P32
Toyosu
豊洲
Maihama
舞浜
Hamamatsucho
浜松町
Tsukiji
築地 P34
Shiodome
汐留
To Shin-
Urayasu
新浦安へ
Tokyo Monorail
東京モノレール
Odaiba
Kaihin Koen
お台場海浜公園
Rinkai Line
りんかい線
TOKYO DISNEY RESORT
東京ディズニーリゾート
Ariake
有明
Odaiba
お台場
Tennouzu Isle
天王洲アイル
Yurikamome
ゆりかもめ
CHINA
Sea of Japan
KOREA
JAPAN
日本
Tokyo
東京
Haneda-
Airport
羽田空港

TOKYO Map 東京中心図
Central TOKYO
Jyujyo 十条
JR Saikyo Line JR埼京線
Oji 王子
Toden Arakawa Line 都電荒川線
Nippori-Toneri Liner 日暮里・舎人ライナー
Tobu Tojyo Line 東武東上線
Oyama 大山
Oku 尾久
Itabashi 板橋
Machiya 町屋
Komagome 駒込
Meiji DORI ST. 明治通り
Sugamo 巣鴨
Tabata 田端
Seibu Ikebukuro Line 西武池袋線
Mejiro DORI ST. 目白通り
Ikebukuro 池袋
Otsuka 大塚
Nishi-Nippori 西日暮里
Shiinamachi 椎名町
Nippori 日暮里
Mejiro 目白
Shimo-Ochiai 下落合
Uguisudani 鶯谷
Seibu Shinjuku Line 西武新宿線
Myogadani 茗荷谷
Ueno Park
Ueno 上野
Takadanobaba 高田馬場
JR Yamanote Line JR山手線
Waseda DORI ST. 早稲田通り
Higashi-Nakano 東中野
Nakano 中野
Waseda 早稲田
Okachi-machi 御徒町
Tokyo Dome
JR Chuo Line JR中央線
Koenji 高円寺
Yamate DORI ST. 山手通り
Iidabashi 飯田橋
Shin-Okubo 新大久保
Akihabara 秋葉原
Okubo 大久保
Seibu-Shinjuku 西武新宿
Imperial Palace
Kan-Nana (Ring7) DORI ST.
Yasukuni DORI ST. 靖国通り
Ichigaya 市ケ谷
Kanda 神田
Shinjuku 新宿
Shinjuku Gyoen National Garden
Yotsuya 四ツ谷
Yoyogi 代々木
Tokyo 東京
Meiji Jingu Shrine
Yurakucho 有楽町
Route 4 Shinjyuku Line 高速新宿線
Jingu Gaien
Sasazuka 笹塚
Keio Line 京王線
Yoyogi Park
Harajuku 原宿
Tokyo Midtown
Meidaimae 明大前
Shimbashi 新橋
Yoyogi-Uehara 代々木上原
Tokyo Tower
Komaba-Todai-mae 駒場東大前
Odakyu Line 小田急線
Shimo-Kitazawa 下北沢
Shibuya 渋谷
Roppongi Hills
Keio Inokashira Line 京王井の頭線
Hamamatsucho 浜松町
Takeshiba 竹芝
Daikanyama 代官山
Ebisu 恵比寿
Tokyu Setagaya Line 東急世田谷線
Hinode 日の出
Nakameguro 中目黒
Tamachi 田町
Sangenjaya 三軒茶屋
Tokyu Toyoko Line 東急東横線
Route 1 Haneda Line 高速羽田線
Route 3 Shibuya Line 高速渋谷線
Meguro 目黒
Gakugeidaigaku 学芸大学
Meguro DORI ST. 目黒通り
Fudomae 不動前
Gotanda 五反田
Shinagawa 品川
Daiba 台場
Komazawa DORI ST. 駒沢通り
Musashi-Koyama 武蔵小山
Dai-Ichi Keihin 第一京浜
Tennouzu Isle 天王洲アイル
Toritsudaigaku 都立大学
Osaki 大崎
Tokyu Meguro Line 東急目黒線
Togoshi-Ginza 戸越銀座
JR Tokaido Shinkansen JR東海道新幹線
Tokyo Monorail
Ooka-yama 大岡山
Jiyugaoka 自由が丘
Hatanodai 旗の台
Oimachi 大井町

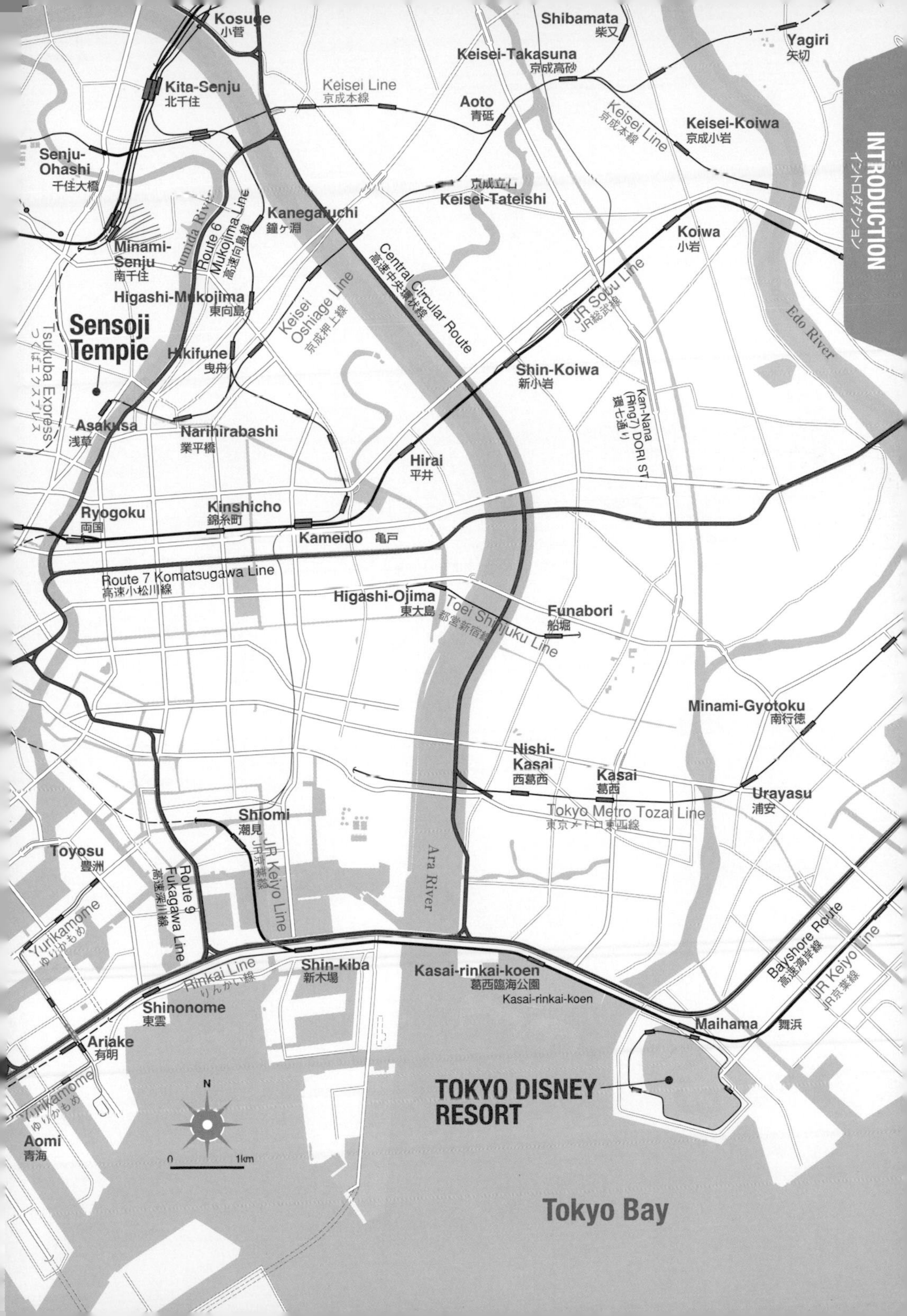
Kosuge
小菅
Shibamata
柴又
Yagiri
矢切
Keisei-Takasuna
京成高砂
Kita-Senju
北千住
Keisei Line
京成本線
Aoto
青砥
Keisei Line
京成本線
Keisei-Koiwa
京成小岩
Senju-Ohashi
千住大橋
京成立石
Keisei-Tateishi
Kanegafuchi
鐘ケ淵
Sumida River
Route 6 Mukojima Line
高速向島線
Koiwa
小岩
Minami-Senju
南千住
Central Circular Route
高速中央環状線
JR Sobu Line
JR総武線
Higashi-Mukojima
東向島
Keisei Oshiage Line
京成押上線
Edo River
Sensoji Tempie
Tsukuba Express
つくばエクスプレス
Hikifune
曳舟
Shin-Koiwa
新小岩
Kan-Nana (Ring7) DORI ST.
環七通り
Asakusa
浅草
Narihirabashi
業平橋
Hirai
平井
Ryogoku
両国
Kinshicho
錦糸町
Kameido 亀戸
Route 7 Komatsugawa Line
高速小松川線
Higashi-Ojima
東大島
Toei Shinjuku Line
都営新宿線
Funabori
船堀
Minami-Gyotoku
南行徳
Nishi-Kasai
西葛西
Kasai
葛西
Urayasu
浦安
Tokyo Metro Tozai Line
東京メトロ東西線
Shiomi
潮見
JR Keiyo Line
JR京葉線
Toyosu
豊洲
Route 9 Fukagawa Line
高速深川線
Ara River
Yurikamome
ゆりかもめ
Rinkai Line
りんかい線
Shin-kiba
新木場
Kasai-rinkai-koen
葛西臨海公園
Kasai-rinkai-koen
Bayshore Route
高速湾岸線
JR Keiyo Line
JR京葉線
Shinonome
東雲
Maihama 舞浜
Ariake
有明
TOKYO DISNEY RESORT
N
Yurikamome
ゆりかもめ
0
1km
Aomi
青海
Tokyo Bay

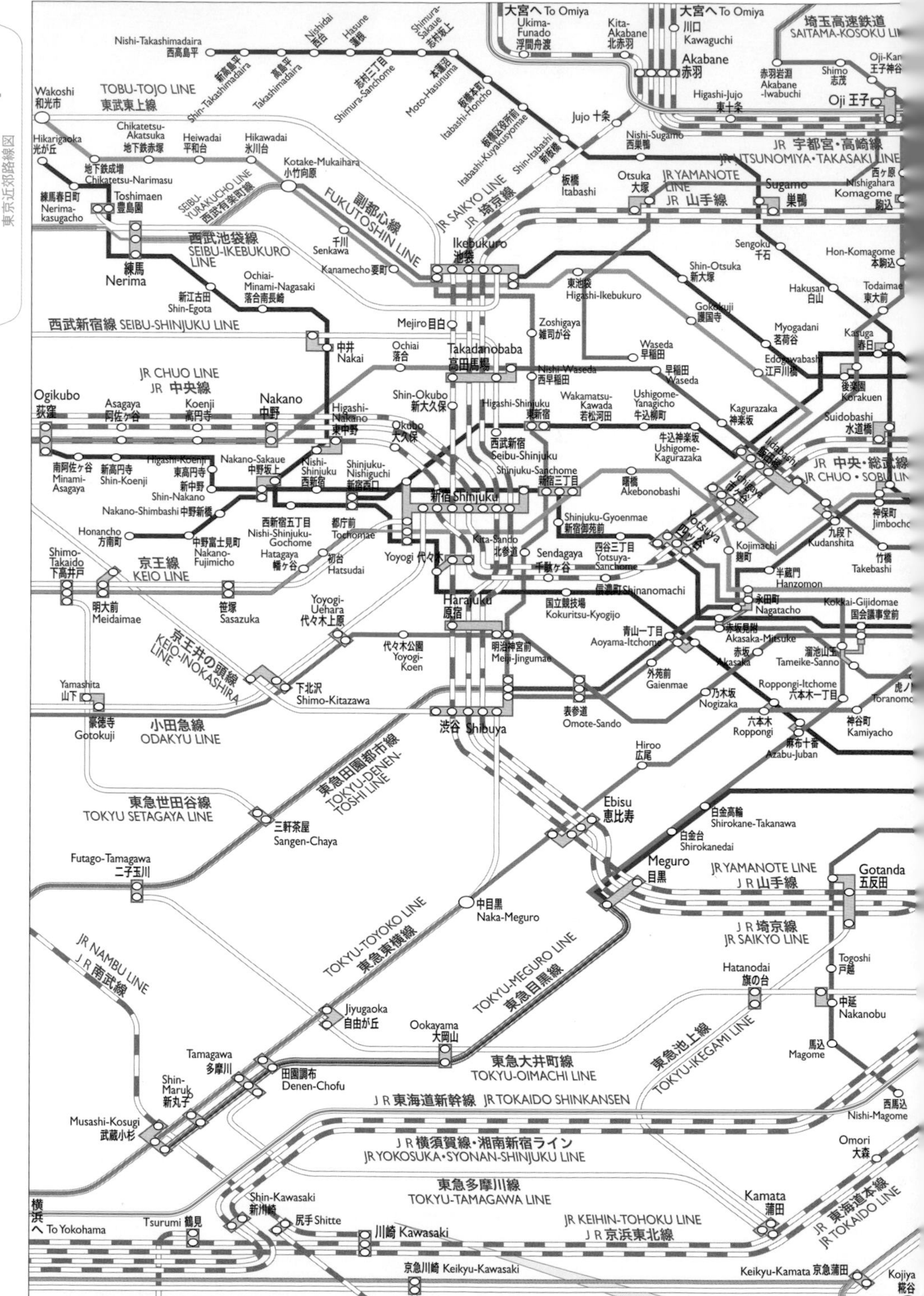
大宮へ To Omiya
Ukima-Funado
浮間舟渡
Kita-Akabane
北赤羽
大宮へ To Omiya
川口
Kawaguchi
Akabane
赤羽
埼玉高速鉄道
SAITAMA-KOSOKU LI
赤羽岩淵
Akabane-Iwabuchi
Shimo
志茂
Oji-Kam
王子神谷
Oji 王子
Higashi-Jujo
東十条
Jujo 十条
Nishi-Sugamo
西巣鴨
JR 宇都宮・高崎線
JR UTSUNOMIYA・TAKASAKI LINE
西ヶ原
Nishigahara
Komagome
駒込
Nishi-Takashimadaira
西高島平
Nishidai
西台
Hasune
蓮根
Shimura-Sakaue
志村坂上
新高島平
Shin-Takashimadaira
高島平
Takashimadaira
志村三丁目
Shimura-Sanchome
本蓮沼
Moto-Hasunuma
板橋本町
Itabashi-Honcho
板橋区役所前
Itabashi-Kuyakusyomae
Shin-Itabashi
新板橋
Wakoshi
和光市
TOBU-TOJO LINE
東武東上線
Hikarigaoka
光が丘
Chikatetsu-Akatsuka
地下鉄赤塚
Heiwadai
平和台
Hikawadai
氷川台
地下鉄成増
Chikatetsu-Narimasu
Kotake-Mukaihara
小竹向原
練馬春日町
Nerima-kasugacho
Toshimaen
豊島園
SEIBU-YURAKUCHO LINE
西武有楽町線
副都心線
FUKUTOSHIN LINE
JR SAIKYO LINE
JR 埼京線
板橋
Itabashi
Otsuka
大塚
JR YAMANOTE LINE
JR 山手線
Sugamo
巣鴨
西武池袋線
SEIBU-IKEBUKURO LINE
練馬
Nerima
千川
Senkawa
Kanamecho 要町
Ikebukuro
池袋
Sengoku
千石
Hon-Komagome
本駒込
Shin-Otsuka
新大塚
東池袋
Higashi-Ikebukuro
Hakusan
白山
Todaimae
東大前
Ochiai-Minami-Nagasaki
落合南長崎
新江古田
Shin-Egota
Gokokuji
護国寺
Zoshigaya
雑司が谷
Myogadani
茗荷谷
Kasuga
春日
西武新宿線 SEIBU-SHINJUKU LINE
Mejiro 目白
中井
Nakai
Ochiai
落合
Takadanobaba
高田馬場
Waseda
早稲田
Edogawabashi
江戸川橋
後楽園
Korakuen
JR CHUO LINE
JR 中央線
Nishi-Waseda
西早稲田
早稲田
Waseda
Ogikubo
荻窪
Asagaya
阿佐ケ谷
Koenji
高円寺
Nakano
中野
Higashi-Nakano
東中野
Shin-Okubo
新大久保
Higashi-Shinjuku
東新宿
Wakamatsu-Kawada
若松河田
Ushigome-Yanagicho
牛込柳町
Kagurazaka
神楽坂
Suidobashi
水道橋
Okubo
大久保
西武新宿
Seibu-Shinjuku
牛込神楽坂
Ushigome-Kagurazaka
Iidabashi
飯田橋
JR 中央・総武線
JR CHUO・SOBU LIN
南阿佐ケ谷
Minami-Asagaya
新高円寺
Shin-Koenji
Higashi-Koenji
東高円寺
新中野
Shin-Nakano
Nakano-Sakaue
中野坂上
Nishi-Shinjuku
西新宿
Shinjuku-Nishiguchi
新宿西口
Shinjuku-Sanchome
新宿三丁目
曙橋
Akebonobashi
Ichigaya
市ケ谷
神保町
Jimbocho
新宿 Shinjuku
Nakano-Shimbashi 中野新橋
西新宿五丁目
Nishi-Shinjuku-Gochome
都庁前
Tochomae
Shinjuku-Gyoenmae
新宿御苑前
Yotsuya
四ツ谷
九段下
Kudanshita
Honancho
方南町
中野富士見町
Nakano-Fujimicho
Hatagaya
幡ケ谷
初台
Hatsudai
Yoyogi 代々木
Kita-Sando
北参道
Sendagaya
千駄ケ谷
四谷三丁目
Yotsuya-Sanchome
Kojimachi
麹町
竹橋
Takebashi
Shimo-Takaido
下高井戸
京王線
KEIO LINE
半蔵門
Hanzomon
信濃町 Shinanomachi
明大前
Meidaimae
笹塚
Sasazuka
Yoyogi-Uehara
代々木上原
Harajuku
原宿
国立競技場
Kokuritsu-Kyogijo
永田町
Nagatacho
Kokkai-Gijidomae
国会議事堂前
赤坂見附
Akasaka-Mitsuke
京王井の頭線
KEIO-INOKASHIRA LINE
代々木公園
Yoyogi-Koen
明治神宮前
Meiji-Jingumae
青山一丁目
Aoyama-Itchome
赤坂
Akasaka
溜池山王
Tameike-Sanno
Yamashita
山下
下北沢
Shimo-Kitazawa
外苑前
Gaienmae
乃木坂
Nogizaka
Roppongi-Itchome
六本木一丁目
虎ノ
Toranomo
豪徳寺
Gotokuji
小田急線
ODAKYU LINE
渋谷 Shibuya
表参道
Omote-Sando
六本木
Roppongi
神谷町
Kamiyacho
麻布十番
Azabu-Juban
Hiroo
広尾
東急田園都市線
TOKYU-DENEN-TOSHI LINE
東急世田谷線
TOKYU SETAGAYA LINE
三軒茶屋
Sangen-Chaya
Ebisu
恵比寿
白金高輪
Shirokane-Takanawa
白金台
Shirokanedai
Futago-Tamagawa
二子玉川
Meguro
目黒
JR YAMANOTE LINE
JR 山手線
Gotanda
五反田
中目黒
Naka-Meguro
JR 埼京線
JR SAIKYO LINE
TOKYU-TOYOKO LINE
東急東横線
JR NAMBU LINE
JR 南武線
TOKYU-MEGURO LINE
東急目黒線
Togoshi
戸越
Hatanodai
旗の台
中延
Nakanobu
Jiyugaoka
自由が丘
Ookayama
大岡山
東急池上線
TOKYU-IKEGAMI LINE
馬込
Magome
Tamagawa
多摩川
東急大井町線
TOKYU-OIMACHI LINE
田園調布
Denen-Chofu
Shin-Maruko
新丸子
JR 東海道新幹線 JR TOKAIDO SHINKANSEN
西馬込
Nishi-Magome
Musashi-Kosugi
武蔵小杉
JR 横須賀線・湘南新宿ライン
JR YOKOSUKA・SYONAN-SHINJUKU LINE
Omori
大森
東急多摩川線
TOKYU-TAMAGAWA LINE
Kamata
蒲田
JR 東海道本線
JR TOKAIDO LINE
横浜
へ To Yokohama
Shin-Kawasaki
新川崎
Tsurumi 鶴見
尻手 Shitte
川崎 Kawasaki
JR KEIHIN-TOHOKU LINE
JR 京浜東北線
京急川崎 Keikyu-Kawasaki
Keikyu-Kamata 京急蒲田
Kojiya
糀谷

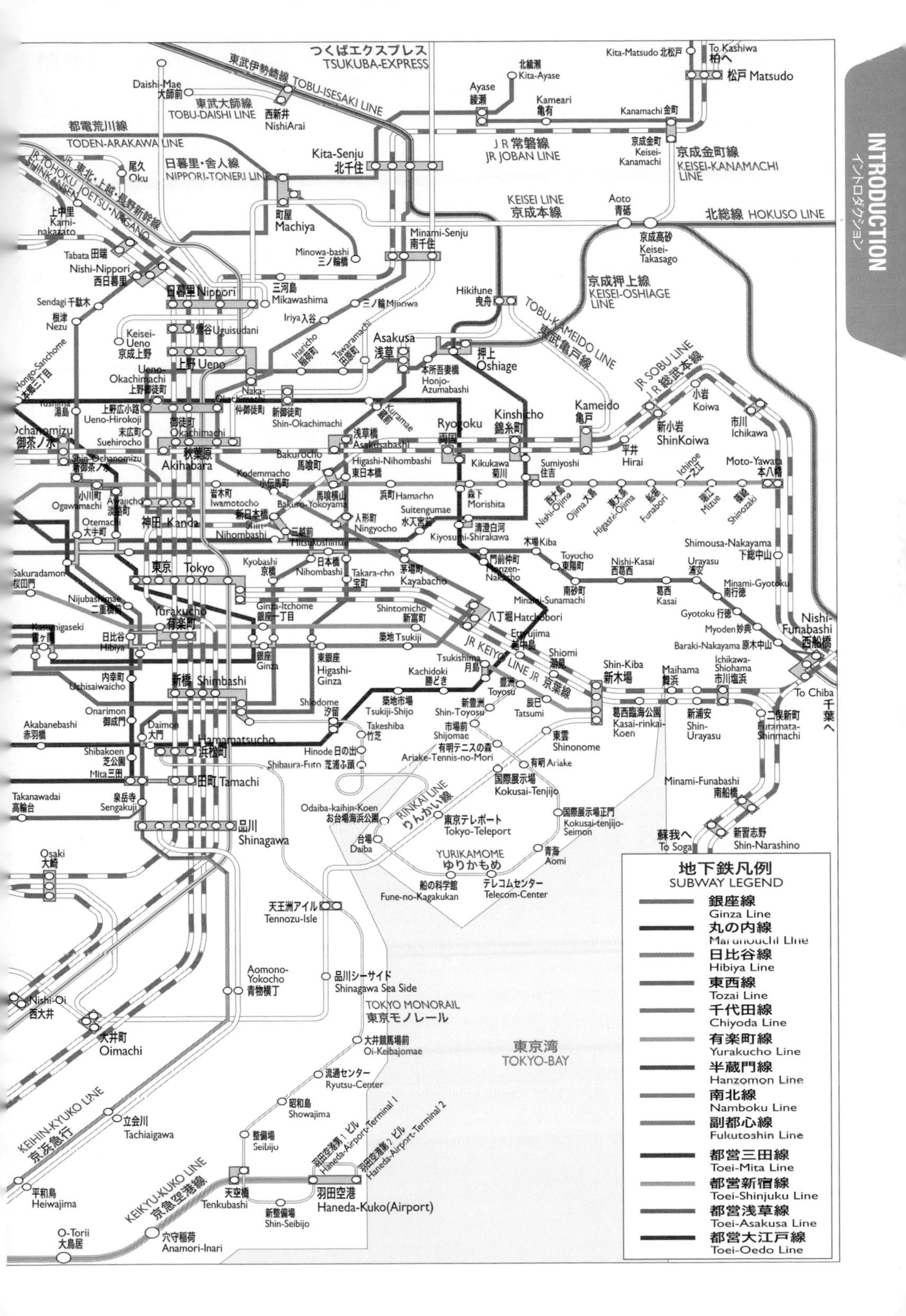
つくばエクスプレス
TSUKUBA-EXPRESS
東武伊勢崎線 TOBU-ISESAKI LINE
Daishi-Mae
大師前
東武大師線
TOBU-DAISHI LINE
西新井
NishiArai
都電荒川線
TODEN-ARAKAWA LINE
JR 東北・上越・長野新幹線
JR TOHOKU JOETSU NAGANO SHINKANSEN
日暮里・舎人線
NIPPORI-TONERI LINE
尾久
Oku
上中里
Kami-nakazato
Tabata 田端
Nishi-Nippori
西日暮里
Sendagi 千駄木
根津
Nezu
Hongo-Sanchome
本郷三丁目
日暮里 Nippori
鶯谷 Uguisudani
Keisei-Ueno
京成上野
上野 Ueno
Ueno-Okachimachi
上野御徒町
Naka-Okachimachi
仲御徒町
Yushima
湯島
上野広小路
Ueno-Hirokoji
末広町
Suehirocho
御徒町
Okachimachi
秋葉原
Akihabara
Ochanomizu
御茶ノ水
Shin-Ochanomizu
新御茶ノ水
小川町
Ogawamachi
Awajicho
淡路町
Otemachi
大手町
神田 Kanda
Sakuradamon
桜田門
東京 Tokyo
Nijubashimae
二重橋前
Kasumigaseki
霞ケ関
日比谷
Hibiya
Yurakucho
有楽町
内幸町
Uchisaiwaicho
新橋 Shimbashi
Onarimon
御成門
Akabanebashi
赤羽橋
Daimon
大門
Shibakoen
芝公園
Mita 三田
Hamamatsucho
浜松町
田町 Tamachi
Takanawadai
高輪台
泉岳寺
Sengakuji
品川
Shinagawa
Osaki
大崎
Nishi-Oi
西大井
大井町
Oimachi
KEIHIN-KYUKO LINE
京浜急行
立会川
Tachiaigawa
平和島
Heiwajima
O-Torii
大鳥居
KEIKYU-KUKO LINE
京急空港線
穴守稲荷
Anamori-Inari
天空橋
Tenkubashi
新整備場
Shin-Seibijo
羽田空港
Haneda-Kuko(Airport)
羽田空港第1ビル
Haneda-Airport-Terminal 1
羽田空港第2ビル
Haneda-Airport-Terminal 2
整備場
Seibijo
昭和島
Showajima
流通センター
Ryutsu-Center
大井競馬場前
Oi-Keibajomae
TOKYO MONORAIL
東京モノレール
品川シーサイド
Shinagawa Sea Side
Aomono-Yokocho
青物横丁
天王洲アイル
Tennozu-Isle
東京湾
TOKYO-BAY
Kita-Senju
北千住
町屋
Machiya
Minami-Senju
南千住
Minowa-bashi
三ノ輪橋
三河島
Mikawashima
三ノ輪 Minowa
Iriya 入谷
Inaricho
稲荷町
Tawaramachi
田原町
Asakusa
浅草
本所吾妻橋
Honjo-Azumabashi
押上
Oshiage
新御徒町
Shin-Okachimachi
Kuramae
蔵前
浅草橋
Asakusabashi
Ryogoku
両国
Bakurocho
馬喰町
Higashi-Nihombashi
東日本橋
Kodemmacho
小伝馬町
岩本町
Iwamotocho
馬喰横山
Bakuro-Yokoyama
浜町 Hamacho
新日本橋
Shin-Nihombashi
三越前
Mitsukoshimae
Nihombashi
人形町
Ningyocho
Suitengumae
水天宮前
Kyobashi
京橋
日本橋
Nihombashi
Takara-cho
宝町
茅場町
Kayabacho
Ginza-Itchome
銀座一丁目
Shintomicho
新富町
八丁堀 Hatchobori
築地 Tsukiji
銀座
Ginza
東銀座
Higashi-Ginza
Shiodome
汐留
築地市場
Tsukiji-Shijo
Kachidoki
勝どき
Tsukishima
月島
Takeshiba
竹芝
Hinode 日の出
Shibaura-Futo 芝浦ふ頭
Odaiba-kaihin-Koen
お台場海浜公園
台場
Daiba
RINKAI LINE
りんかい線
東京テレポート
Tokyo-Teleport
YURIKAMOME
ゆりかもめ
船の科学館
Fune-no-Kagakukan
テレコムセンター
Telecom-Center
青海
Aomi
国際展示場正門
Kokusai-tenjijo-Seimon
国際展示場
Kokusai-Tenjijo
有明 Ariake
有明テニスの森
Ariake-Tennis-no-Mori
市場前
Shijomae
新豊洲
Shin-Toyosu
豊洲
Toyosu
辰巳
Tatsumi
東雲
Shinonome
Hikifune
曳舟
TOBU-KAMEIDO LINE
東武亀戸線
Kinshicho
錦糸町
Kameido
亀戸
Kikukawa
菊川
Sumiyoshi
住吉
森下
Morishita
清澄白河
Kiyosumi-Shirakawa
門前仲町
Monzen-Nakacho
木場 Kiba
Toyocho
東陽町
南砂町
Minami-Sunamachi
Etchujima
越中島
Shiomi
潮見
JR KEIYO LINE JR 京葉線
Shin-Kiba
新木場
葛西臨海公園
Kasai-rinkai-Koen
Maihama
舞浜
新浦安
Shin-Urayasu
Ichikawa-Shiohama
市川塩浜
二俣新町
Futamata-Shinmachi
Nishi-Kasai
西葛西
葛西
Kasai
Urayasu
浦安
Minami-Gyotoku
南行徳
Gyotoku 行徳
Myoden 妙典
Baraki-Nakayama 原木中山
Nishi-Funabashi
西船橋
To Chiba
千葉へ
Minami-Funabashi
南船橋
新習志野
Shin-Narashino
蘇我へ
To Soga
西大島
Nishi-Ojima
Ojima 大島
東大島
Higashi-Ojima
船堀
Funabori
Ichinoe
一之江
瑞江
Mizue
篠崎
Shinozaki
Moto-Yawata
本八幡
Shimousa-Nakayama
下総中山
平井
Hirai
新小岩
ShinKoiwa
小岩
Koiwa
市川
Ichikawa
JR SOBU LINE
JR 総武本線
京成押上線
KEISEI-OSHIAGE LINE
Aoto
青砥
京成高砂
Keisei-Takasago
KEISEI LINE
京成本線
北総線 HOKUSO LINE
京成金町
Keisei-Kanamachi
京成金町線
KEISEI-KANAMACHI LINE
Kanamachi 金町
JR 常磐線
JR JOBAN LINE
Ayase
綾瀬
北綾瀬
Kita-Ayase
Kameari
亀有
Kita-Matsudo 北松戸
To Kashiwa
柏へ
松戸 Matsudo
地下鉄凡例
SUBWAY LEGEND
銀座線
Ginza Line
丸の内線
Marunouchi Line
日比谷線
Hibiya Line
東西線
Tozai Line
千代田線
Chiyoda Line
有楽町線
Yurakucho Line
半蔵門線
Hanzomon Line
南北線
Namboku Line
副都心線
Fukutoshin Line
都営三田線
Toei-Mita Line
都営新宿線
Toei-Shinjuku Line
都営浅草線
Toei-Asakusa Line
都営大江戸線
Toei-Oedo Line

Kaminari-mon

Asakusa
浅草

Your royal road to a glimpse of “Japan”

"ニッポン"観光の王道

Ikebukuro
Ginza Line
Ueno
Asakusa
Shinjuku
Chūō Line
Shibuya
Tokyo
Yamanote Line
Shinagawa

Asakusa has flourished as one of Tokyo’s leading entertainment districts since the pleasure quarters and playhouses of the Edo period, and the area still features old-world Japanese charm. You can see Tokyo’s oldest temple, Sensoji Temple, as well as the stores that line Nakamise and Denbouin-dori St. offering souvenirs from Japan’s past. Enjoy eel, tempura, and dojo fish dishes at restaurants with long-standing reputations.

江戸時代から遊郭や芝居小屋が集まる東京随一の盛り場として栄え、現在でも下町の雰囲気が漂う。東京で最古の寺院・浅草寺をはじめ、昔ながらのみやげもの店が軒を連ねる仲見世通りや伝法院通りが見どころ。うなぎ、天ぷら、どじょうなどの老舗の味も魅力。

Sensoji Temple

Jinrikisha

Search for Edo-style souvenirs at Nakamise

仲見世で探す江戸みやげ

Around 90 stores line the 250-meter street from the Kaminari-mon Gate to the Hozo-mon Gate of Sensoji Temple.

雷門から浅草寺宝蔵門まで、長さ250mの通りに約90店舗が並ぶ

Nakamise-dori St.

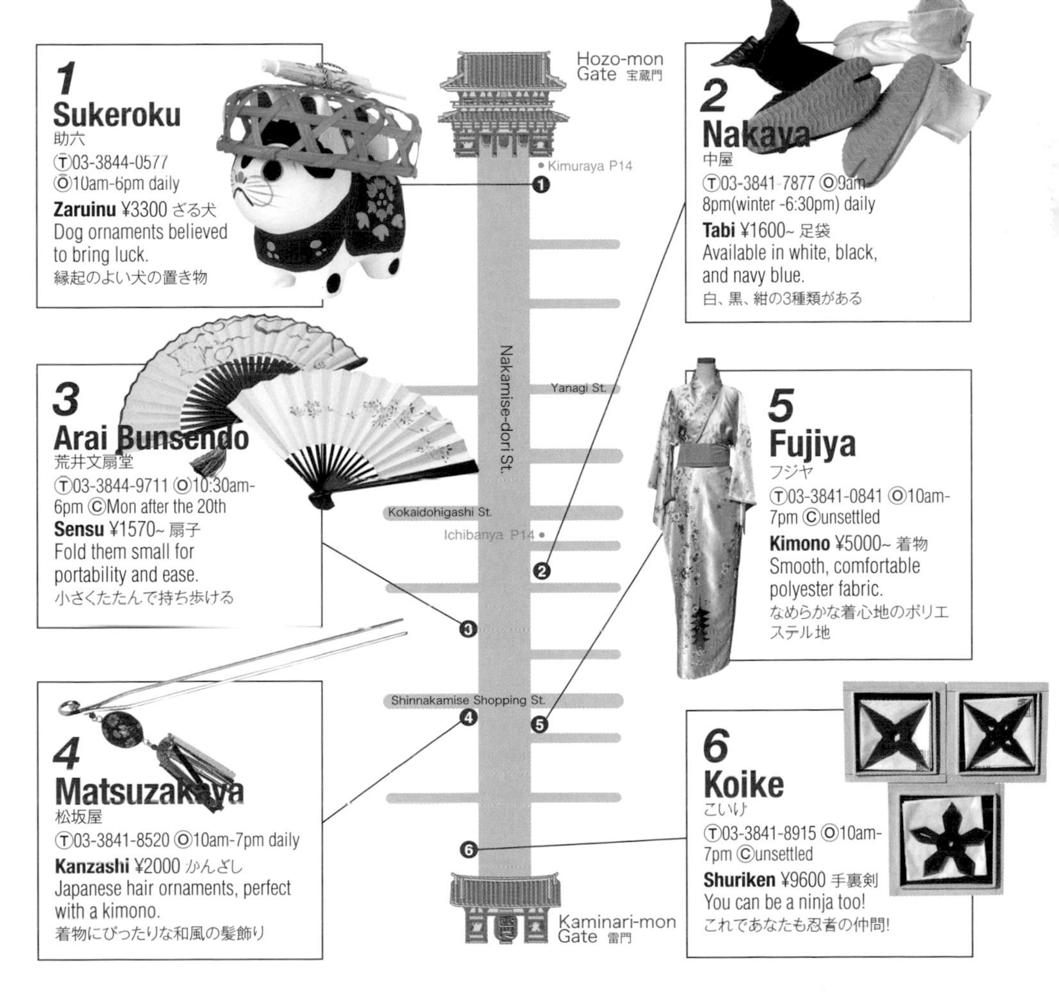

1 Sukeroku

助六

Ⓣ03-3844-0577 Ⓞ10am-6pm daily

Zaruinu ¥3300 ざる犬
Dog ornaments believed to bring luck.
縁起のよい犬の置き物

2 Nakaya

中屋

Ⓣ03-3841-7877 Ⓞ9am-8pm(winter -6:30pm) daily

Tabi ¥1600~ 足袋
Available in white, black, and navy blue.
白、黒、紺の3種類がある

3 Arai Bunsendo

荒井文扇堂

Ⓣ03-3844-9711 Ⓞ10:30am-6pm ⒸMon after the 20th

Sensu ¥1570~ 扇子
Fold them small for portability and ease.
小さくたたんで持ち歩ける

5 Fujiya

フジヤ

Ⓣ03-3841-0841 Ⓞ10am-7pm Ⓒunsettled

Kimono ¥5000~ 着物
Smooth, comfortable polyester fabric.
なめらかな着心地のポリエステル地

4 Matsuzakaya

松坂屋

Ⓣ03-3841-8520 Ⓞ10am-7pm daily

Kanzashi ¥2000 かんざし
Japanese hair ornaments, perfect with a kimono.
着物にぴったりな和風の髪飾り

6 Koike

こいけ

Ⓣ03-3841-8915 Ⓞ10am-7pm Ⓒunsettled

Shuriken ¥9600 手裏剣
You can be a ninja too!
これであなたも忍者の仲間!

The charm of Asakusa's long-established stores

浅草老舗の味

1 "Dojo" fish

どぜう

Established 207 years ago. Enjoy folk cuisine from the Edo period while dining in gallery seating. ¥1650

創業207年。江戸時代の庶民料理「どぜう」が桟敷席で食べられる。

Komakata dojo
Ⓣ03-3842-4001 Ⓞ11am-9pm daily

2 Anmitsu

あんみつ

Very popular with women, Umezono boasts a wide range of sweets such as traditional Anmitsu bean paste and sweet millet soups. Anmitsu¥682

女性ファンが多い、あんみつや粟ぜんざいなどの甘味が揃う。

Umezono
Ⓣ03-3841-7580 Ⓞ10am-8pm Ⓒunsettled

3 Tempura

天ぷら

Famous for their large, satisfying kakiage fritters with prawn and scallops. ¥3150

海老と貝柱を使った、ボリューム満点のかき揚げが名物。

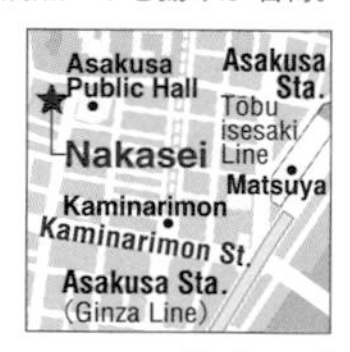

Nakasei
Ⓣ03-3841-4015 Ⓞ11:30am-2pm,5pm-10pm ⒸTue,Second and Fourth Mon

4 Unagi (eel)

うなぎ

200 years of cherished tradition. Enjoy dining while gazing over the Sumidagawa River. ¥2310~

200年の伝統を守る老舗。隅田川を眺めながら食事ができる。

Maekawa
Ⓣ03-3841-6314 Ⓞ11:30am-8:30pm daily

For itinerant gourmands…

食べ歩きグルメ

Sembei

せんべい

Asakusa's famous sembei rice crackers are hand-grilled over charcoal fires by professionals, one by one. ¥50~

職人が一枚ずつ炭火で焼き上げる浅草名物の手焼せんべい。

Ichibanya
Ⓣ03-3842-5001
Ⓞ9am-7pm daily
Map p13

Ningyoyaki

人形焼

Filled with sweet anko bean paste, these sponge cakes are formed into dolls and other shapes. ¥500(8pieces)

人形などをかたどったカステラの中に餡が入っている。

Kimuraya
Ⓣ03-3844-9754
Ⓞ9:30am-6:30pm daily Map p13

Kappabashi: Japan's leading kitchen implement and cutlery district

日本一の道具街·かっぱ橋

An amazing array of specialty stores for cooking wares and kitchen implements is located in these streets. You can walk here from Asakusa.

調理・厨房備品の専門店が集まる商店街。浅草から歩いて行ける。

Kappabashi-dori St.

1 Sushi keyholder

寿司サンプルのキーホルダー

Salmon roe and tuna sushi; so real you'll want to take a bite! ¥950

思わず食べたくなるイクラとマグロ

2 Folding chopsticks

折りたたみ箸

You can also have your name carved to order. ¥2300~

注文すれば名前を彫ってくれる

1 **Sato Sample**
サトウサンプル
Ⓣ03-3844-1650 Ⓐ3-7-4 Nishi-Asakusa, Taito-ku Ⓞ9am-6pm Ⓒunsettled

2 **Takemura**
竹むら
Ⓣ03-3841-4362
Ⓐ1-10-8 Moto-Asakusa, Taito-ku Ⓞ9am-6pm
ⒸSun

3 **Tanaka Shikkiten**
田中漆器店
Ⓣ03-3841-6755 Ⓐ1-9-12 Matsugaya,Taito-ku Ⓞ9am-5:30pm
ⒸSun,National Holiday

4 **Yabukita**
やぶきた
Ⓣ03-3842-2221 Ⓐ1-4-8 Nishi-Asakusa,Taito-ku
Ⓞ9am-5:30pm Ⓒ Sun,National Holiday

5 **Saito**
さいとう
Ⓣ03-3841-5260
Ⓐ2-12-6 Matsugaya, Taito-ku Ⓞ9am-5:30pm
ⒸSun, National Holiday

3 Lacquerware small box

漆の小箱

Lacquerware boxes with many uses for small objects. ¥2940

用途豊富な小物入れ

4 Chopstick rests

箸置き

Rest your chopsticks on the curves of these broad beans. ¥525

そら豆の凹みに箸を置く

3 Lacquer wan bowl

漆器椀

The beautiful patterns of Japan. ¥3108

和風の柄が美しい

5 Noren fabric divider

暖簾

Decorate the entrance to any room. ¥3300

部屋の入り口に飾ってみては

Akihabara 秋葉原

Sacred ground for "otaku" geeks

世界のオタクの聖地

One of the world's pre-eminent electronics quarters, handling all kinds of electrical goods from household appliances and computers to wireless devices, Akihabara is also renowned as a gathering place for "otaku" geeks from all over the world. Here you will find countless anime DVD and figurine shops, maid cafes where customers are greeted by costumed waitresses, and more.

家電、パソコンから無線機器まで、あらゆる電気製品が揃う世界有数の電気街であるとともに、今や世界中から「オタク」が集う街として有名。アニメのDVDやフィギュアのショップ、コスチューム姿の女の子が出迎えてくれるメイドカフェなどが街中にあふれている。

"Akiba(Akihabara)-style" B-class dining

アキバ的B級グルメ

Cheap fast foods with a pop-culture edge: perfect for a stroll around town.

街歩きのお供にぴったりな、チープでポップなファーストフード。

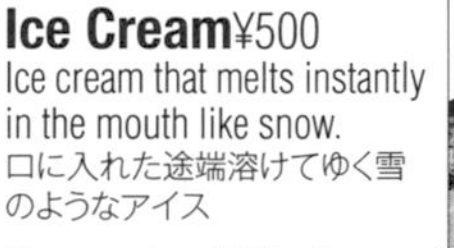

Ice Cream ¥500
Ice cream that melts instantly in the mouth like snow.
口に入れた途端溶けてゆく雪のようなアイス

Dragon Ice Akihabara The Head Store
Ⓣ03-3256-2505 Ⓐ3-15-6 Sotokanda, Chiyoda-ku
Ⓞ11am-7pm Ⓒunsettled

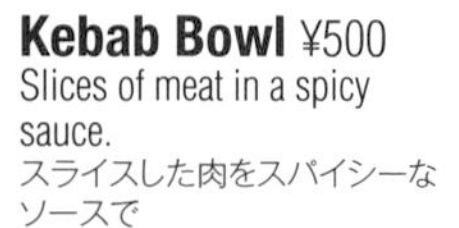

Kebab Bowl ¥500
Slices of meat in a spicy sauce.
スライスした肉をスパイシーなソースで

STAR KEBAB Akiba Terrace
Ⓣ03-3255-0004
Ⓐ3-10-7 Sotokanda, Chiyoda-ku
Ⓞ10am-9:30pm daily

Pasta Can ¥300
Ramen Can ¥300
Unique canned pasta and noodles.
パスタやラーメンなどのユニークな缶詰

Chichibu Denki
Ⓣ03-3253-3443 Ⓐ3-12-15 Sotokanda, Chiyoda-ku
Ⓞ10:30am-7:30pm daily

Interested in cosplay?

コスプレしよう!

Express your love by getting into a favorite character. National holidays in Akiba are for cosplay shows!

キャラになりきることで愛情を表現。休日のアキバはコスプレショー!

Akihabara is the paradise for costume player!
アキバはコスプレのパラダイスです♪

School uniform of Rei Ayanami, heroine of Evangelion. ¥10290
エヴァンゲリオンのヒロイン、綾波レイが通う学校の制服

Enjoy our housemaid costume.
私たちのメイド服も楽しんでね!

T-shirt featuring the popular Gundam character Dozle. ¥3045
ガンダムの人気キャラクター、ドズルがTシャツに

T-shirt featuring famous quotes of Gundam character Gihren. ¥3045
ガンダムのギレンの名台詞をプリントしたTシャツ

Costume from the popular anime "ARIA". ¥52500
人気アニメ「ARIA」のコスチューム

You can see various character.
いろんなキャラクターに逢えるよ

to Ueno
GEE! STORE AKIBA
Laox ASO BIT CITY
Chuō St.
JR Yamanote・Keihintōhoku Line
JR Sōbu Line
Akihabara Sta.

GEE! STORE AKIBA
Ⓣ03-3526-6877
Ⓞ11am-8pm daily

What is "MOE"?
"萌え"って何?

This term expresses a feeling. The meaning is close to "cute," but it is used to discuss a fictional anime or game characters.
感情を表す言葉。「可愛い」に近いが、その対象がアニメやゲームの架空のキャラクターなどの場合に用いる。

Experience a maid cafe!

メイドカフェ初体験!

The cafe that grants an obscure wish: to be greeted by a cute maid upon returning home.

「家に帰るとかわいいメイドさんがいたら…」そんな夢が叶うカフェ

1 First, the greeting: "Oh, welcome, sir!"
「いらっしゃいませご主人様!」とお出迎え

2 Placing an order offers the chance for conversation.
オーダーの時が会話のチャンス

3 The maid brings your order with unique voice and mannerisms.
独特の仕草と声で注文の品を運んできてくれる

4 Table service also available.
テーブルでのサービスもある

Maid Cafe Pinafore
Ⓣ03-5846-0778
Ⓞ11am-10pm daily

You can try this here, too!
ここでも体験できる

A Japanese-style interior and kimono-clad maid.
和風の店内で、メイドさんは着物姿。

@ home café Hana
Ⓣ03-5294-7709
Ⓞ11:30am-10pm daily

Maid cafe in the daytime, the maids transform into a game or anime characters at the nighttime.
昼のメイド、夜はゲームやアニメのキャラに変身。

Cafe mai:lish
Ⓣ03-5289-7310 Ⓞ11am-10pm daily

Infiltrate an otaku shop

オタクショップに潜入

Get a high-tech robot!
ハイテクロボットをゲット!

Figures

フィギュア

Choose the pose as you wish. ¥1995
自由にポーズが決められる

For the interior of the room
お部屋のインテリアに

The directly managed store of Kaiyodo, known world-wide as a maker of various fine figures.
数々の名作フィギュアで世界的に知られる海洋堂の直営店。

Kaiyodo Hobby Lobby Tokyo
Ⓣ03-3253-1951
Ⓞ11am-8pm
ⒸWed

Robot

ロボット

Popular 2-legged walking robot.
人気の二足歩行ロボット

This specialty store handles kits and parts for home-made robots. ¥80000~
自作ロボットのキットからパーツまでを扱う専門店。

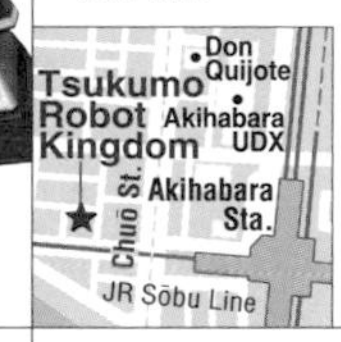

Tsukumo Robot Kingdom
Ⓣ03-3251-0987
Ⓞ10:30am-8pm (Sun,Holiday-7:30pm) daily

Akiba souvenirs

アキバみやげ

Cookie with maid illustration. ¥500
メイドイラストのクッキー

Confectionery, character merchandise, maid costumes, and a great deal more: these make ideal souvenirs of Akihabara.
お菓子やキャラクターグッズ、メイド服などを秋葉原みやげに。

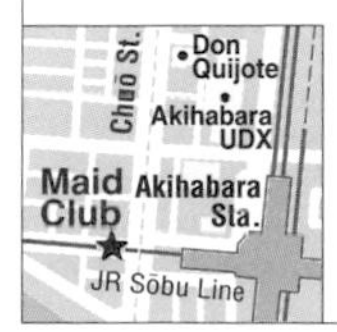

Maid Club
Ⓣ03-3251-3557
Ⓞ11am-8pm daily

Idol merchandise

アイドルグッズ

Matching T-shirts as "idols". ¥3000
アイドルとお揃いのTシャツを

Concerts are held daily, the concept being "idols you can go and meet".
「会いに行けるアイドル」をコンセプトに日々公演を行う。

AKB48 theater
Ⓣ03-5298-8648
Ⓞ7pm(Sat, Sun, Holiday 1pm-,6pm-) daily Ⓕ¥3000

Character merchandise

キャラクターグッズ

Face towel from the anime "Keroro Gunso (Sgt. Frog)". ¥600
アニメ「ケロロ軍曹」のフェイスタオル

©吉崎観音／角川書店 サンライズ・テレビ東京・NAS

Apart from Japanese anime exhibitions and events, there is also an ample selection of shops here.
日本アニメの展示、イベントなどを行うほか、ショップも充実。

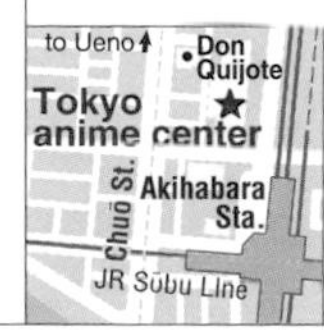

Tokyo anime center
Ⓣ03-5298-1188
Ⓞ11am-7pm
Ⓒunsettled

六本木 Roppongi

Where cutting edges meet

最先端が集まる街

With the opening of Roppongi Hills in 2003 and Tokyo Midtown in 2007, Roppongi has become Tokyo's most popular tourist destination. Both these complexes boast numerous designer fashion stores and high-class restaurants in conjunction with art galleries. The area's time-honored clubs and bars still keep Roppongi nights alive and kicking.

2003年に六本木ヒルズが、2007年に東京ミッドタウンがオープン。いずれも流行のブランドショップや高級レストランが出店する複合施設で、美術館も併設。今や東京で一番観光客が集まる街となった。昔ながらのクラブやバーなど、夜の六本木もまだまだ健在。

Tokyo Midtown

Tokyo Midtown

東京ミッドタウン

Since its opening in March 2007, Midtown has garnered attention as Tokyo's hottest spot to watch. Around 130 stores have premises here.

2007年3月オープンの東京で今一番注目のスポット。約130の店舗が入る

Art

Suntory Museum of Art

サントリー美術館

The collection centers on objects for daily furnishing goods: paintings, ceramics, glass, and more.

絵画、陶芸、ガラスなど、生活調度品を中心にしたコレクション。

Ⓣ03-3479-8600
Ⓞ10am-6pm(Wed to Sat -8pm) ⒸTue
Ⓕaccording to program

Garden

Midtown Garden

ミッドタウン・ガーデン

Park located on the site of the old Defense Agency. The broad expanse of lawn is dotted with artworks.

防衛庁の跡地にある公園。広い芝の上にはアート作品が点在する。

Restaurant

Kafka

可不可

Japanese restaurant in collaboration with top Japanese creators such as Kashiwa Sato

佐藤可士和など日本のトップクリエーターとコラボレートする和食店。

Ⓣ03-5413-7700
Ⓞ11am-midnight daily

Roppongi Hills

六本木ヒルズ

Having opened in April 2003, Roppongi Hills is almost a self-contained town comprising an art gallery, a movie theater, and around 230 stores.

2003年4月オープン。美術館や映画館ほか店舗数は約230と、一つの街のよう

Tokyo City View on the 52nd floor of the Mori Tower

Mori Tower, Roppongi Hills

Symbol of Roppongi, "town of art"

「アートの街・六本木」のシンボル

Japan's fifth national art institution opened in January 2007. The on-site restaurant is also very popular. Lunch ¥1800~

2007年1月オープンの日本で5番目の国立美術館。館内のレストランも人気。ランチコース¥1800～。

The National Art Center, Tokyo

Ⓣ03-5777-8600 Ⓞ10am-6pm(Fri - 8pm) ⒸTue Ⓕaccording to program

Art

Mori Art Museum

森美術館

Art museum on the 53rd floor of the Mori Tower, symbol of Roppongi Hills.

六本木ヒルズのシンボル、森タワー53階にある現代アートの美術館。

Ⓣ03-5777-8600 Ⓞ10am-10pm(Tue - 5pm) Ⓒunsettled Ⓕaccording to program

Garden

Mouri Garden

毛利庭園

A verdant Japanese garden built on the site of an Edo-period daimyo lord's mansion

江戸時代の大名屋敷跡に作られた緑豊かな日本庭園。

Ⓞ7am-11pm

Shop

LE CHOCOLAT DE H

ル ショコラ ドゥ アッシュ

Chocolate specialist store operated by top pâtissier Hironobu Tsujiguchi

トップパティシエ、辻口博啓が手がけるショコラ専門店。

Ⓣ03-5772-0075 Ⓞ11am-8pm daily

Hotel

Grand Hyatt Tokyo

グランド ハイアット 東京

Located within Roppongi Hills, Grand Hyatt Tokyo is a "Lifestyle Destination Hotel".

六本木ヒルズ内にある、究極のライフスタイルを追求した"デスティネイションホテル"。

Ⓣ03-4333-1234

六本木ナイト

Roppongi Night

Your highway to Tokyo nightlife

東京夜遊びの王道

Roppongi crossing

Experience Roppongi by night: go clubbing until dawn or maybe take in a newhalf show!

朝まで踊れるクラブやニューハーフ·ショーが楽しめる店など、夜の六本木へいざ！

Drag show pub

ショーパブ

Glamorous drag queens present a fabulous dance show on an elaborate stage.

美しいニューハーフが大仕掛けの舞台でダンスショーを繰り広げる。

ROPPONGI KAGUWA
Ⓣ03-5414-8818
Ⓞ6pm-4am(Sun,Tue to Thu 6pm-12:30am)
ⒸMon Ⓕ¥3500

Pub

パブ

A genuine British pub, with draft beer imported directly from the UK. Hobgoblin Dark Ale ¥1000

イギリス直輸入の生ビールが飲める本場のブリティッシュ·パブ。ホブゴブリンダークエール1000円。

HOBGOBLIN Roppongi
Ⓣ03-3568-1280
Ⓞ5pm-1am(Sat, Sun, Holiday 11pm~) daily

Enjoy the night!
夜を楽しもう!

Live music
ライブハウス

Enjoy world-class dining while listening to performances by world-class artists.
世界的なアーティストの演奏を聴きながら極上の食事を

Billboard Live TOKYO
Ⓣ03-3405-1133
Ⓞaccording to program
Ⓒunsetlled Ⓕaccording to program

Club
クラブ

Indispensable for all-night partying. Wide non-genre music selection means that anyone can have a great time.
夜遊びの定番。ノージャンルな選曲で誰でも気軽に楽しめる。

CLUB & LOUNGE FLOWER
Ⓣ03-5785-1761
Ⓞ8pm-
ⒸMon,Tue,Thu,Sun
Ⓕaccording to program

Beatles live show
ビートルズライブ

Live performances of famous Beatles songs. Fans attend from across the globe.
ビートルズの名曲をライブ演奏。世界中からファンが訪れる。

CAVERN CLUB
Ⓣ03-3405-5207 Ⓞ6pm-2:30am(Holiday 12am) daily
Ⓕ¥1890

Sports bar
スポーツバー

Showing world major sports events on 7 screen.Like Legends double burger ¥1800,extensive American food menu are available.
世界中のスポーツを7つのスクリーンで堪能。レジェンズ・ダブルバーガー1800円などアメリカンなフードメニューも充実。

Legends Sports Bar
Ⓣ03-3589-3304 Ⓞ17pm-1am daily

Shinjuku 新宿

Tokyo's largest terminal

東京屈指の巨大ターミナル

Isetan Sinjukuten

A diverse cityscape centers on Shinjuku station, which welcomes more commuters per day than any other station in Japan. Tokyo tocho (Tokyo Metropolitan Government Buildings) and a forest of skyscrapers can be found in the office district by the west entrance, while the east entrance features a concentration of famous department stores and youth-oriented shops, as well as one of Japan's leading entertainment districts in Kabuki-cho. With the remarkable re-development of the south entrance, it all adds up to a swirling and sometimes chaotic sense of energy.

１日の乗降客数日本一を誇る新宿駅を中心に多様な街並みが広がる。都庁をはじめ、高層ビルが林立するオフィス街の西口、有名デパートや若者向けのショップが集中し、日本有数の歓楽街、歌舞伎町を擁する東口、再開発著しい南口など、混沌としたパワーが渦巻く。

Ikebukuro
Ueno
Shinjuku
Chūō Line
Shibuya
Tokyo
Yamanote Line
Shinagawa

A superb view from Tokyo tocho

東京都庁で絶景を

Standing 45 stories and 202 meters tall, Tokyo tocho also features two observation decks (on the north and the south) which can be used free of charge.

地上202m、45階に無料で利用できる南北2つの展望室がある。

Tocho souvenirs

都庁みやげ

Exclusive to Tokyo. Tocho Kitty strap ¥420
東京限定。都庁キティのストラップ

Tocho manju (bean paste bun) ¥1050
都庁まんじゅう

Tokyo Metropolitan Government Buildings
Ⓣ03-5321-1111
Ⓞ9:30am-11pm daily

Experience the art of Japan 日本の芸能を体験

There are many places to enjoy Japanese entertainment such as traditional Yose variety shows, Enka music, and more.

伝統的な寄席や演歌など、日本発のエンタメを楽しめる場所が多い。

Yose variety shows

寄席

As well as yose such as Rakugo storytelling, you can also enjoy arts such as Manzai comedy, conjuring acts, acrobatic acts, and more.
落語をはじめとした寄席のほか、漫才や奇術、曲芸などが楽しめる。

Shinjuku Suehirotei
Ⓣ03-3351-2974
Ⓞ12pm-4:30pm, 5pm-9pm
Ⓕ¥2700

Manzai comedy

漫才

You can view live performances by celebrities from the Yoshimoto Kogyo group, well-known from television appearances.
テレビでもお馴染み、吉本興業の人気芸人によるライブが見られる。

LUMINE the Yoshimoto
Ⓣ03-5339-1112
Ⓞ11am-9:30pm (Sat, Sun, National Holiday 10:30pm-) daily Ⓕ¥4000

TV Studio Audience

番組観覧

The long-running comedy program Waratte Iitomo ("it's okay to laugh") broadcasts live in studio Alta. Advance bookings required.
スタジオアルタでは長寿番組「笑っていいとも」を生放送。要事前申込。

Studio ALTA

Enka music and stage performance

演歌と舞台

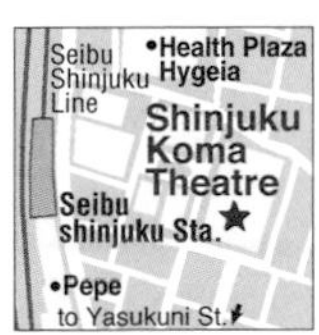

This massive theater seats 2092. You can catch theatrical shows and performances by renowned enka singers here.
客席数2092の大劇場。大物歌手の演歌や芝居が堪能できる。

Shinjuku Koma Theatre
Ⓣ03-3200-2213
Ⓞaccording to the performance daily
Ⓕaccording to program

Kabukicho 歌舞伎町

Kabukicho never sleeps!

24時間眠らない街

One of World's most renowned entertainment districts, extending from the north entrance of Shinjuku station, Kabukicho is packed with theaters, cinemas, restaurants, and adult entertainment businesses.

新宿駅の北側に広がる世界有数の歓楽街。劇場や映画館、飲食店、風俗店が密集している。

Kabukicho Ichiban-gai A

歌舞伎町一番街

This is the main street of Kabukicho, which continues towards the Koma Stadium from Yasukuni-dori.

靖国通りからコマ劇場前へ続く歌舞伎町のメインストリート。

Cabaret club

キャバクラ

At these establishments, patrons mingle with female hostesses known as "cabaret club ladies."

「キャバクラ嬢」と呼ばれる女性スタッフが接待してくれる飲食店。

Host club

ホストクラブ

Good-looking male "hosts" do their best to cater to the female guests.

イケメン男性が女性客に対して、至れり尽くせりの接待をする。

Club Ai

Ⓣ03-3208-6435
Ⓞ5:30pm-1am daily
Ⓕ¥5000(2hr. first time)

Ramen as a mop-up

Nothing hits the spot like ramen after a late night of drinking! Ramen ¥700~ (Kamukura)
お酒を飲んだ後に食べる深夜のラーメンはこのうえない美味! ラーメン¥700~(神座)

Kamukura
Ⓣ03-3209-3790
Ⓞ11am-8am daily

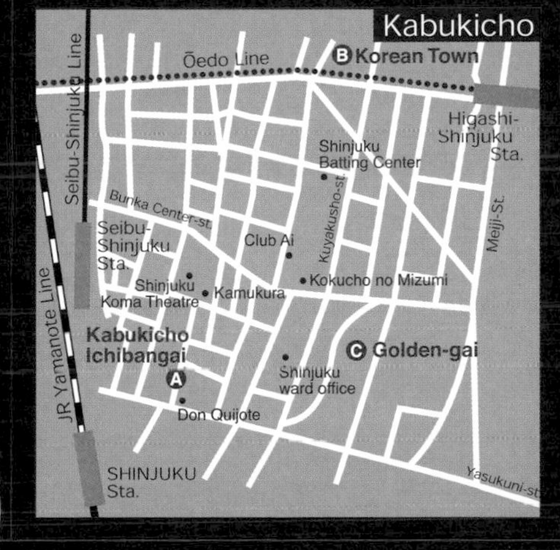

Omotesando

Harajuku/ Omotesando

原宿・表参道

Design & fashion district 流行ファッションの街

Omotesando, a beautiful avenue of keyaki zelkova trees, marks the main approach to Meiji-jingu Shrine. High-class designer stores, such as those at the landmark Omotesando Hills, line the way. Takeshita-dori of Harajuku, where high school students throng, Ura-Harajuku (Ura-Hara) area, where cutting-edge street-fashion stores are dotted... This area is always at the center of attention.

ケヤキ並木が美しい表参道は明治神宮御苑への参道。街のランドマーク、表参道ヒルズをはじめ、高級ブランドのショップが立ち並ぶ。中高生で賑わう原宿・竹下通り、時代をリードするストリートブランドのショップが点在する裏原宿と、注目のエリアが集まる。

Search for knick-knacks down Takeshita-dori.

竹下通りで雑貨探し

Packed with cheap, cute items. Massively popular with high school students!

中高生も大好きな、チープでかわいいものがいっぱい！

You might think it's a beer bottle, but it's actually a clock! ¥399
ビール瓶かと思ったら、時計です

1

Wander the streets, crepe in hand! ¥200~
クレープ片手にお店めぐり

2

1 Zona Liberata Harajuku
Ⓣ03-3403-9848
Ⓐ1-16-4 Jingu-mae,Shibuya-ku
Ⓞ10:30am-8pm daily

2 Marion Crepe
Ⓣ03-3401-7297
Ⓐ1-6-15 Jingu-mae,Shibuya-ku
Ⓞ10:30am-8pm daily

Meiji Shrine

Check out Harajuku-originated designer brands.

原宿発ブランドをチェック

The stores in the "Ura-Hara" area (the back streets of Harajuku) are hugely popular with stylish young people.

オシャレな若者に絶大な人気、「裏原」（原宿の裏通り）エリアのショップ

BAPE STORE® HARAJUKU

ベイプ ストア ハラジュク

The brand, with its trademark ape head, was started up by designer NIGO® in 1993.

1993年にNIGO®が立ち上げたブランド。猿の顔がトレードマーク。

Ⓣ03-5474-0204
Ⓞ11am-7pm daily

Shoes ¥17640

T-shirts ¥6090

NEIGHBORHOOD

ネイバーフッド

A unique mix of motorcycle, military, and work items is a popular theme here.

バイク、ミリタリー、ワークをミックスさせた独自のアイテムが人気。

Ⓣ03-3401-1201
Ⓞ12am-8pm daily

T-shirts ¥13650

Shirts ¥16800

HEAD PORTER TOKYO

ヘッド ポーター トウキョウ

Original bags are functional and good looking.

機能性とデザイン性に優れたオリジナルバッグを中心に販売。

Ⓣ03-5771-2621
Ⓞ12am-7pm ⒸWed

Bag ¥14700～

Lamp harajuku

ランプ ハラジュク

A select shop handling mainly fashion items from Japanese designers.

日本人デザイナーのファッションアイテムを中心に扱うセレクトショップ。

Ⓣ03-5411-1230
Ⓞ12am-8pm daily

Shoes ¥19950

Bag ¥26250

Shibuya 渋谷

The epicenter of youth culture
若者文化の発信地

Hachiko

Located near the fashion quarters of Harajuku and Daikanyama, Shibuya is full of fashion, gourmet, movies, and music hotspots to hold the interest of teens and twentysomethings. Watch a dizzying tide of human movement wash across the famous pedestrian crossing in front of Shibuya station. If you want to get a handle on Japan's youth culture, look no further than Shibuya!

ファッションやグルメ、映画や音楽など、10代から20代の若者の関心を集めるスポットが集まる街。ファッションの街・原宿や代官山からも近く、有名な駅前スクランブル交差点は人の流れで目まいがしそうなほど。日本の若者文化を知りたければ、シブヤに行こう！

A local landmark
街のランドマーク

SHIBUYA 109
SHIBUYA 109
The symbol of Shibuya fashion
渋谷ファッションのシンボル

Shibuya Seibu
シブヤ西武
A large department store, comprising A and B buildings
A館とB館がある大型デパート

Marui City Shibuya
マルイシティ渋谷
A long-established Shibuya fashion department store
渋谷では老舗のファッションデパート

SHIBUYA MARK CITY
渋谷マークシティ

Contains shops, restaurants, and a hotel
ショップ、レストラン、ホテルが入る

QFRONT
QFRONT
The building has a massive and distinctive video screen
ビル前面の巨大ビジョンが目印

Shibuya PARCO
渋谷PARCO

PARCO has numerous premises located around this area.
周辺に複数の店舗を展開する

What did you come to Shibuya to do today?

今日はシブヤに何しにきたの？

We asked young people in Shibuya.

To go around the select shops

セレクトショップめぐりに

Jinnan district is best for stylish stores, isn't it?
オシャレな店なら神南界隈ですね

To catch a movie

映画を見に

To watch art-style single-theater movie, Shibuya is a must.
単館上映のアート作品なら渋谷です

To check out new CDs

新譜CDのチェックに

Well, Tower & HMV are must-go.
タワーとHMVはとりあえずマスト

TOWER RECORDS Shibuyaten
TOWER RECORDS 渋谷店
Ⓣ03-3496-3661
Ⓐ1-22-14 Jinnan, Shibuya-ku
Ⓞ10am-23pm
Ⓒunsettled

HMV Shibuya
HMV 渋谷
Ⓣ03-5458-3411
Ⓐ24-1 Udagawacho, Shibuya-ku
Ⓞ10am-23pm daily

Just to hang out at a cafe

カフェでまったりしに

There are more quiet cafes here than you thought.
静かなカフェも意外に多いんです

To party at clubs

クラブに遊びに

To party all night in any spaces; from obako (large-scale house) to kakurega (hideout-style)!
大バコから隠れ家系までオールで遊べる!

Shopping at 109

109でショッピング

To pick up some style ideas from shop attendants
店員さんのスタイルがお手本です

Ginaza Mitsukosi

Matsuya Ginza

Ginza 銀座

Shopping district on Japan's most expensive real estate

地価日本一のショッピングエリア

Ginza boasts a history dating from the Meiji period. Long-established businesses, renowned department stores, and the world's most distinguished designer stores, as well as restaurants and high-class clubs, line the streets of this sophisticated and charming downtown area. The streets are arranged along a handy grid pattern; easy to memorize, and on festivals and holidays the main street is opened up as a paradise for pedestrians.

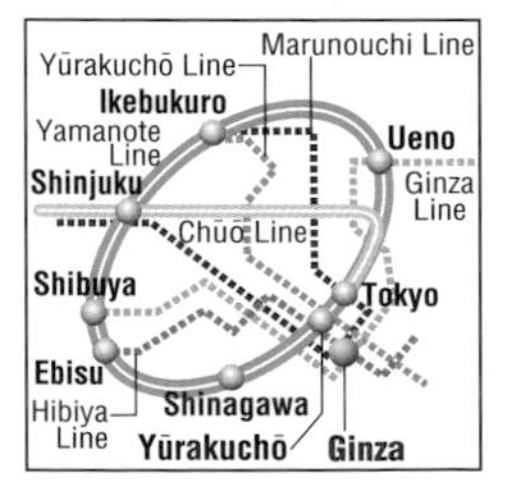

明治時代からの歴史ある商業地。老舗商店に有名デパートが立ち並び、世界中の一流ブランドが出店する洗練された町並みが魅力。飲食店や高級クラブも多い。通りは碁盤の目状なので覚えやすく、休日にはメインストリートの中央通りが歩行者天国として開放される。

Ginza: Designer shopping district

ブランドの街、銀座

Like New York's 5th Avenue or the Champs-Elysées in Paris, many world-class designer fashion stores such as Dior and Tiffany's have gathered in this area, principally around Chuo-dori and Namiki-dori streets.

ニューヨークの5番街、パリのシャンゼリゼのように、中央通り、並木通りを中心に、ディオール、ティファニーといった世界のスーパーブランドが集結している。

Dior Ginza

Wandering the long-established stores of Ginza

銀座の老舗めぐり

Tokyo Kyukyodo

東京鳩居堂

This specialist store for incense, small articles, knick-knacks, and calligraphy supplies has been in business since Japan's Edo period.

江戸時代から続くお香や和小物、和雑貨、書画用具の専門店。

Ⓣ03-3571-4429 Ⓞ10am-7:30pm daily

Incense set made with shell ¥3150
貝を使った香立セット

For storing small objects. Shaped like the footwear of maiko(apprentice geisha).¥420
舞妓さんの履物型小物入れ

Ginza Ito-ya

銀座・伊東屋

The leading stationery department store in Japan. A huge array of items can be found both in the main building and the annex.

日本を代表する文房具のデパート。本館と別館に豊富な品揃えを誇る。

Ⓣ03-3561-8311 Ⓞ10:30am-8pm daily

A red paperclip, the symbol of the store ¥315
店のシンボル、赤いクリップ

You can have your name inlaid into this leather business card case ¥4725
名入れも可能な牛皮の名刺入れ

Kimuraya Sohonten Ginza

木村屋總本店 銀座本店

This bakery, founded 139 years ago, was the originator of the anpan bun, which features red bean paste inside sweet pastry.

パンの中に餡が入った「あんぱん」を考案した、創業139年のパン店。

Ⓣ03-3561-0091 Ⓞ10am-9pm daily

The quintessential anpan red bean paste bun ¥137
定番の桜あんぱん

Koransha

香蘭社

Manufacturers of serving dishes and interior articles. The silver & gold-painted lazuline glaze is known as Koransha cho (style).

器やインテリアを製造。金銀彩のルリ釉は「香蘭社調」と呼ばれる。

Ⓣ03-3543-0951
Ⓞ9:30am-6pm
ⒸSun, National Holiday

Large dish, Aka-e (red pincture) of Arita ware ¥3675
有田焼の「赤絵」大皿

Lazuline glaze photo frame ¥5250
ルリ釉のフォトフレーム

Ginza Lion

ライオン 銀座七丁目店

Retro atmosphere
レトロな雰囲気

A beer hall with over 70 years of history and tradition. The draft beer has a solid reputation.

70年を超える歴史と伝統をもつビヤホール。生ビールが絶品と評判。

Ⓣ03-3571-2590 Ⓞ11:30am-11pm daily

築地 Tsukiji

Head out to Tsukiji market

築地市場に出かけよう

Renowned as Japan's largest fish market, Tsukiji market is a publicly-operated wholesale market also dealing in fruit, vegetables, and other foodstuffs. With an indoor market where the professionals bid, as well as an outdoor market packed with retail stores, Tsukiji also features fishmongers, dried goods stores, and restaurants using these fresh ingredients, all open to the public. Remember your manners while looking around inside!

日本最大の魚市場として有名な築地市場は、青果などの食材も扱う公設の卸売市場。プロのセリが行われる場内市場と小売店が軒を連ねる場外市場に分かれ、一般客が利用できる鮮魚や乾物店、新鮮な食材を使った飲食店もある。場内見学はマナーを守って行おう。

Tsukiji market

Indispensable in the preparation of sushi, the tuna on display at Tsukiji comes from across the globe.
世界中から築地に集まるマグロは、寿司には欠かせないネタ。

Miyako
みやこ
Every single section of tuna is available at specialist stores.100g￥1000～
専門店にはマグロのあらゆる部位が揃う。
Ⓣ03-3547-6622 Ⓐ4-13-13 Tsukiji,Chuo-ku Ⓞ8am-3pm ⒸSun,National Holiday

Tour around inside Tsukiji market

築地市場場内を見学

The inner market, containing bidding area and wholesalers, conveys a bustling professional feeling.

セリ場や仲卸がある場内市場で、プロの活気を感じてみよう。

Turret, the transporter used in the market
市場内で使われる運搬車、ターレ

SIGHTSEEING エリア別観光

Hirayama-syoten

平山商店

A collection of original Tsukiji memorabilia patterned with fish illustrations and kanji characters.
魚の絵柄や漢字をデザインした築地オリジナルの商品が揃う。

Ⓣ03-3541-6586 Ⓞ3am-2pm
ⒸSun,National Holiday

Face cloth ¥420~
てぬぐい

Fish kanji T-Shirt ¥1575
魚漢字Tシャツ

Hunting cap ¥2625
ハンチング帽

Toyo-chan

豊ちゃん

There's always a queue outside this Western-style restaurant. Well-known dishes include katsu-don and katsu curry.
いつも行列の洋食店。カツ丼やカツカレーなど名物料理が多数。

Ⓣ03-3541-9062 Ⓞ5:30am-1:30pm
ⒸSun,National Holiday

Katsu-Don ¥990
カツ丼

Tenfusa

天房

Prawns, whiting, peppers, and more: such generous portions, they stick out of the bowl!
海老、キス、シシトウなど、丼からはみ出るほどのボリューム。

Ⓣ03-3547-6766 Ⓞ6:30am-2pm
ⒸSun,National Holiday

Ten-Don ¥1000
天丼

Daiwa-zushi

大和寿司

Its prime location inside the market gives you a taste of the freshest seafood.
市場内にあるので、仕入れたばかりの新鮮なネタが味わえる。

Ⓣ03-3547-6807
Ⓞ5:30am-1:30pm
ⒸSun,National Holiday

Omakase Sushi ¥3500
おまかせ握り

Ueno Park

Ueno 上野

A forest of art and some great bargains

アートの森と激安の街

Ueno is Tokyo's northern gateway; the Shinkansen bullet train departs from and arrives here. Sightseers gather from all over Japan to visit Ueno Park, famed for its cherry trees. The park also contains many significant galleries and museums, as well as a zoo. The Ameyoko shopping district runs alongside the elevated railway on the south side of Ueno station. You can find anything - fashion, household items, foodstuffs - at cheap prices in this shopper's paradise.

新幹線が発着する東京の北の玄関口。桜の名所として有名な上野公園には、有数の美術館や博物館、動物園などがあり、全国から観光客が集まる。駅南側の高架に沿って伸びる商店街"アメ横"は、ファッションから日用品、食品まで安価で入手できる買い物天国。

Statue of Saigo Takamori (Ueno Park)

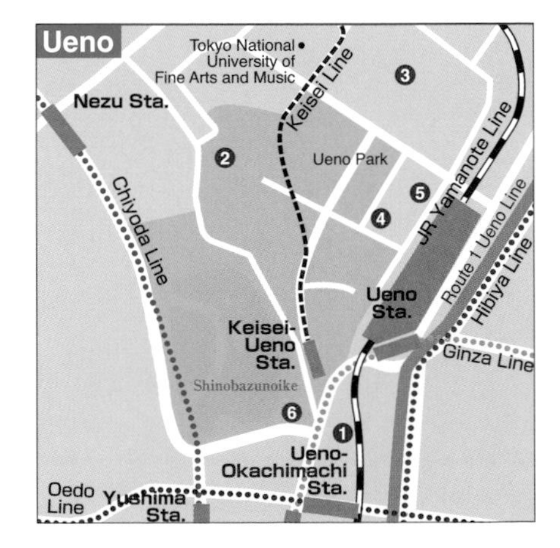

1
Ameyoko
アメ横

All kinds of bargains can be found along this street: from food supplies to clothes and cosmetics.
食料品から衣料、コスメなど、様々な激安店が軒を連ねる通り。

Cosmetics are also extremely cheap here
化粧品も激安価格

You will find many fishmongers here
鮮魚店も多い

2
Ueno Zoological Gardens
上野動物園

Founded in 1882, Ueno Zoological Garden has the longest history of any zoo in Japan. Around 3200 animals of 500 species are kept here.
明治15年（1882）開園の日本で最も歴史ある動物園。約500種、3200頭の動物を飼育。

Ⓣ03-3828-5171 Ⓞ9:30am-5pm ⒸMon Ⓕ¥600

Ling Ling the panda
パンダのリンリン

3
Tokyo National Museum
東京国立博物館

More than 110 thousand Japanese and Asian artworks and ancient relics are stored here, many of them national treasures.
日本や東洋の美術品、考古遺物11万点以上を所蔵。国宝も多数。

Ⓣ03-5777-8600 Ⓞ9:30am-5pm ⒸMon Ⓕ¥600

A lot of treasures

The much-loved haniwa clay figure exhibition
人気の埴輪の展示

4
The National Museum of Western Art, Tokyo
国立西洋美術館

This museum houses and exhibits Western artworks, some dating back to the Middle Ages. See Monet, Renoir, and more.
モネ、ルノワールなど、中世以降の西洋美術を収蔵・展示。

Ⓣ03-5777-8600 Ⓞ9:30am-5:30pm ⒸMon Ⓕ¥420

The building was designed by Le Corbusier
建物はル・コルビュジエによる設計

5
National Science Museum
国立科学博物館

Over ten thousand items on display, spanning all the natural sciences: life sciences, environmental sciences, outer space, and more.
生命と地球環境、宇宙など自然科学全般にわたり1万点以上を展示。

Ⓣ03-5777-8600 Ⓞ9am-5pm ⒸMon Ⓕ¥600

6
Shitamachi Museum
台東区立下町風俗資料館

A recreation of downtown shitamachi districts from the Meiji period to the Showa period. There is also an exhibition where you can actually handle the items.
明治から昭和にかけての下町を再現。実際に触れられる展示もある。

Ⓣ03-3823-7451 Ⓞ9:30am-4:30pm ⒸMon Ⓕ¥300

谷中·根津 Yanaka/ Nezu

Popular for strolls through old Tokyo streets

人気の下町散歩道

Dotted with temples and shrines, this area is popular for nostalgic strolls and viewing old wooden architecture; many structures have been standing for over 100 years. The Japanese way of life from days long past is still evident here, visible in the long alleyways lined with narrow-fronted row houses, the many named hills and stairways, and the traditional malls where local residents mingle, It's a great spot to stroll and feel a traditional Japanese atmosphere.

数多くの寺社が点在し、築100年を超える木造建築が残るノスタルジックな町並みが人気。長屋が続く細い路地に、名前が付いた坂道や階段、地元の人で賑わう商店街など、ひと昔前の日本の暮らしが息づく、下町の雰囲気を感じながら散策しよう。

Yuyake Dandan

Old-fashioned back alleys
昔ながらの路地裏

Yanaka Ginza

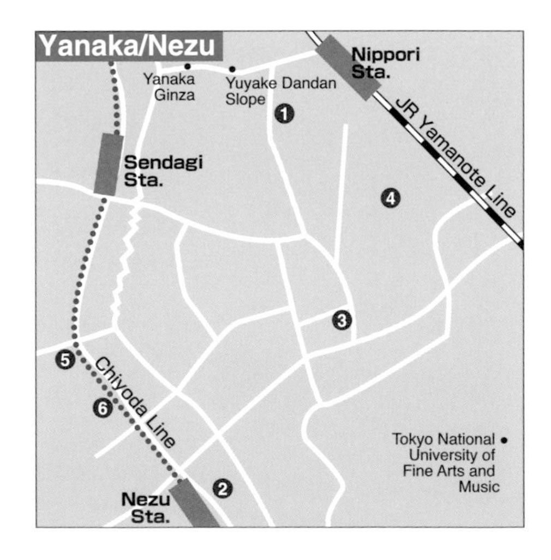

1 Asakura Choso Museum

朝倉彫塑館

Exhibition of works in the home/atelier of sculptor the late Fumio Asakura

彫刻家、故朝倉文夫の自宅兼アトリエに作品を展示。

Ⓣ03-3821-4549 Ⓞ9:30am-4pm
ⒸMon,Fri Ⓕ¥400

2 Kushiage-dokoro Hantei

くしあげどころ はん亭

Enjoy kushi-age (skewered & fried) seafood, meat, and vegetables in this building dating from the Meiji period.

明治時代の建物で、魚介や肉、野菜などの串揚げが食べられる。

Ⓣ03-3828-1440 Ⓞ11:30pm-2pmLO, 5pm-9:30pmLO ⒸMon

3 SCAI THE BATHHOUSE

スカイ ザ バスハウス

An art space in a converted bathhouse, with exhibitions of works by domestic and foreigh artists

元銭湯を利用したアートスペース。国内外の作家の作品を展示。

Ⓣ03-3821-1144 Ⓞ12pm-7pm
ⒸSun,Mon,National Holiday

4 Yanaka Cemetery

谷中霊園

Many famous people are interred here, such as Yoshinobu Tokugawa, the last shogun of the Tokugawa family.

徳川家最後の将軍、徳川慶喜をはじめ、多くの著名人が眠る墓地。

Ⓣ03-3821-4456

5 Nezu Shrine

根津神社

At the Edo period, the largest shrine structure in the town. A main hall and 7 outlying buildings are specified as important cultural properties.

江戸時代、市中最大の神社建築で、本殿ほか7棟が重要文化財。

Ⓣ03-3822-0753 Ⓞ6am-5pm daily

6 Nezu no Taiyaki

根津のたいやき

Taiyaki are shaped like fish and filled with sweet red bean paste. People queue for taiyaki from this perennial favorite. ¥140

たいやきは魚型の皮の中に餡が入ったお菓子。行列のできる人気店。1個140円。

Ⓣ03-3823-6277 Ⓞ10:30am-until sold out Ⓒunsettled

Nijyu-bashi leading to the main gate

皇居 The Imperial Palace

A quiet oasis in the heart of the city

都心に広がるオアシス

Stronghold of the Tokugawa shoguns during the Edo period, the Imperial Palace is the current residence of the Emperor of Japan. Despite its location in the heart of Tokyo, broad green space still prevails here. There are many historical sights, such as the remains and gardens of Edo Castle and exhibitions of artworks handed down within the Imperial household. While some areas are open to general admission, viewing some other areas will require booking in advance.

江戸時代は徳川将軍の居城であり、現在は天皇の住居。東京の中心にありながら広大な自然が残る。江戸城の遺構や庭園、皇室に受け継がれてきた芸術品の展示など、歴史的な見どころも多い。一般に公開されているエリアと事前申し込みで見学できるエリアがある。

Kyuden

Ⓣ03-3213-1111
(for visit reservation)

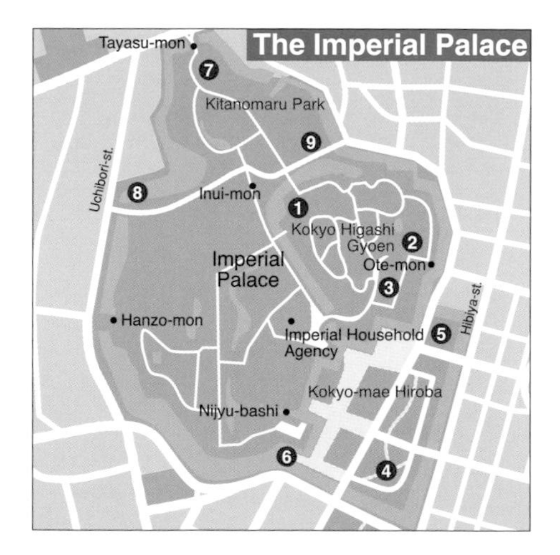

Kokyo Higashi Gyoen

皇居東御苑

History area where look of Edo Castle is left

江戸城の面影を残す歴史エリア　ⓞ9am-4:30pm ⓒMon, Fri

1 Edojyo Tensyukaku-ato

江戸城天守閣跡

Only the stonewall foundation remains of castle tower now.

現在は基盤であった石垣だけが残る。

2 Sannomaru shozokan

三の丸尚蔵館

The artworks housed in the Imperial Palace are exhibited here.

皇室が収蔵する美術品を展示。

3 Hyakunin Bansho

百人番所

This was the Edo Castle guardhouse.

江戸城の警備所だったところ。

Kokyo-mae Hiroba

皇居前広場

Oasis area enclosed by moat

濠に囲まれたオアシスエリア

4 Bronze statue of Masashige Kusunoki

楠正成像

Bronze statue of this hero from the Nambokucho (Northern and Southern Courts) period.

南北朝時代の英雄の銅像。

5 Wadakura Fountain Park

和田倉噴水公園

The symbolic fountain shoots water as high as 8.5 meters.

8.5mも水を噴き上げる噴水がシンボル。

6 Sakurada-mon

桜田門

Famous as the venue of certain historical event.

歴史的な事件の舞台として有名。

Kitanomaru Park

北の丸公園

Cultural facilities and rest spots are scattered

文化施設や憩いのスポットが点在

7 Nippon Budokan

日本武道館

This martial arts sanctuary is also famed as a venue for concerts.

武道の殿堂。コンサート会場としても有名。

8 Chidorigahuchi Boat Arena

千鳥ヶ淵ボート場

Ride on a boat in the Imperial Palace moat.

皇居のお濠でボートに乗ることができる。

ⓞ11am-5:30pm ⓒDec-Feb ⓕ¥500(30min).

9 The National Museum of Modern Art, Tokyo

東京国立近代美術館

This Museum houses modern and contemporary Japanese artworks.

日本の近・現代美術作品を所蔵。

ⓣ03-5777-8600 ⓞ10am-5pm ⓒMon ⓕ¥420

Tokyo Tower
東京タワー

Symbol of Tokyo in both past and present
今も昔も東京のシンボル

333m!

Tokyo Tower was constructed as a radio tower in 1958. The observation deck 150 meters above the ground affords a panoramic view throughout the Kanto area. The building at its base contains amusements and other facilities.

　1958年に完成した電波塔。地上150mにある展望台からは関東一円が一望できる。足元のビルにはアミューズメント施設などが入る。

Tokyo Tower
Ⓣ03-3433-5111
Ⓞ9am-10pm daily Ⓕ Main Obsevatry¥820, Special Obsevatry+¥600

The view from the special observation deck
特別展望台からの眺め

Check this out too!
ここもチェック！

Eagle Tower ¥450

Souvenir floor
おみやげフロア

A collection of 17 souvenir stores
みやげ店17店舗が集まっている。
2F Ⓞ9am-10pm

Wax figure gallery
蝋人形館

A huge array of wax figures imported directly from London
ロンドン直輸入の蝋人形がずらり。

3F Ⓞ10am-9pm Ⓕ¥500

Guinness world record museum TOKYO
ギネス・ワールド・レコード・ミュージアム TOKYO

Presenting records accredited by Guinness World Records
ギネスに認定された記録を紹介。

4F
Ⓞ10am-9pm
Ⓕ¥700

国会議事堂

National Diet Building

The heart of Japanese politics 日本の政治の中心

The Japanese Diet comprises the Lower and Upper Houses of Diet. This building is where the Members of Diet represent the Japanese people. Construction of the building, built symmetrically along the left-right axis, was completed in 1936. The Upper House is located on the right side, and the Lower House is located on the left side.

国会は衆議院と参議院で構成され、国民の代表が議員を務める。1936年に完成した建物は左右対称の造りで右が参議院、左が衆議院。

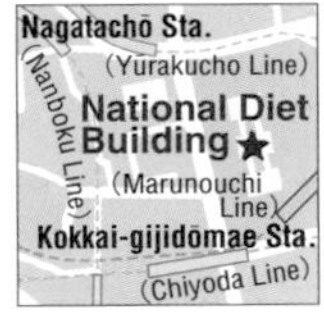

National Diet Building
Ⓣ03-3581-3100 (Councilors Telephone Service) Ⓞ9am-4pm Ⓒ Sat, Sun, National Holiday

You can tour around inside free of charge.

内部を無料で見学できる

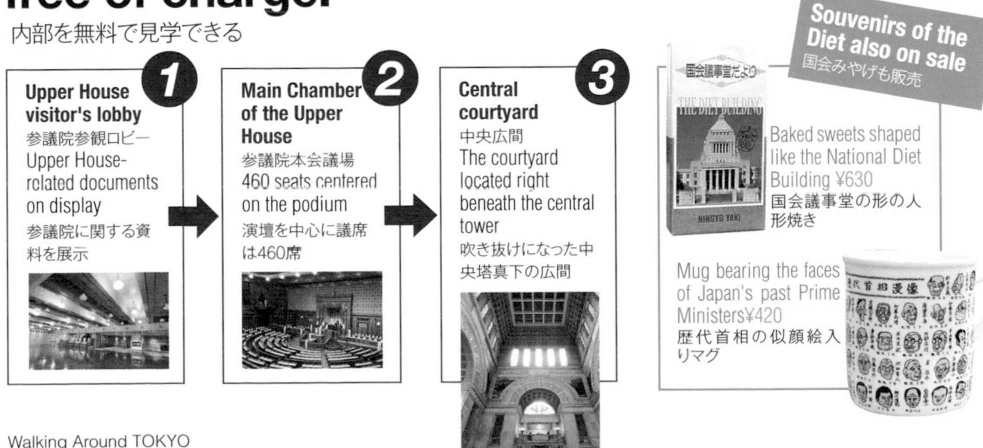

日本庭園

Japanese Garden

Steeped in traditional Japanese beauty

日本伝統の美に浸る

Happoen

Many Japanese gardens are maintained for public admission, even within the heart of Tokyo, in such places as temples, hotels, or the ex-mansions of feudal lords. These include "pond circuit" gardens designed for viewing while strolling around a central pond, as well as Zen-influenced karesansui "dry" gardens that use sand and rock to express mountain and water. These enable you to experience a refined beauty that is unique to Japan.

東京都心では、大名屋敷の跡地や寺院、ホテルなどにあり、公園として整備されているものも多い。池を中心とした散策路を歩きながら鑑賞する「池泉回遊式」、禅の影響下にあり、砂や石などで山水を表現する「枯山水」など、日本独特の繊細な様式美が鑑賞できる。

Japanese garden highlights

日本庭園の見どころ

Flowers
花
A sense of the seasons: cherry blossoms in spring, hydrangeas in the rainy season
春の桜、梅雨のアジサイなどで季節を感じよう

Bridges 橋
Many kinds of stone or wooden bridges, some with covered roofs
石橋や木橋に屋根付きのものなど様式はさまざま

Stone lantern
石灯籠
Originally pillars for housing lanterns, in Japanese gardens these are meant to be viewed
元は灯りをともす台だが、庭園のものは鑑賞用

Pond 池
You stroll around the central pond to appreciate it.
庭の中心に配され、周囲を歩きながら鑑賞する

Garden stones
庭石
The Japanese style emphasizes placement of unprocessed natural stones.
天然石を加工せずに配置するのが日本式

Trees
庭木
Species and placement of trees are carefully considered.
木の種類や植える場所などは計算されている

Guide to Tokyo gardens

東京名園ガイド

Shinjyukugyoen
新宿御苑

Originally created as a garden for the Imperial Palace.
元は皇室の庭園として造られた。

ⓉO3-3350-0151 Ⓐ11 Naitoucho, Shinjuku-ku Ⓞ9am-4pm ⒸMon Ⓕ¥200

Happoen
八芳園

Previously the mansion of a daimyo lord.The beautifulgarden is now used for wedding ceremonies.
元大名屋敷の、庭の美しい結婚式場。

Ⓣ03-3443-3111 Ⓐ1-1-1 Shiroganedai, Minato-ku Ⓞunsettled

Koishikawakourakuen
小石川後楽園

Completed by Mito Mitsukuni, known affectionately as Komon-sama.
「黄門様」の愛称の水戸光圀が完成させた。

Ⓣ03-3811-3015 Ⓐ1-6-6 Kouraku, Bunkyo-ku Ⓞ9am-5pm daily Ⓕ¥300

Kiyosumiteien
清澄庭園

A garden circuit, situated around a central pond and pine trees.
池や松を中心とした回遊式庭園。

Ⓣ03-3641-5892 Ⓐ3-3-9 Kiyosumi, Koto-ku Ⓞ9am-4:30pm daily Ⓕ¥150

Rikugien
六義園

It derives its motifs from the scenery described in classic Man'yo shu poetry
「万葉集」などで詠まれた風景がモチーフ。

Ⓣ03-3941-2222 Ⓐ6-16-3 Honkomagome, Bunkyo-ku Ⓞ9am-5pm daily Ⓕ¥300

HamarikyuGarden
浜離宮恩賜庭園

Scenery changes by the sea ebbs and flows
海水の干満により風景が変化する。

Ⓣ03-3541-0200 Ⓐ1-1 Hamarikyuteien Chuo-ku Ⓞ9am-5pm daily Ⓕ¥300

Kyuyasudateien
旧安田庭園

A promenade, rich in scenery, surrounds the pond.
池の周りを変化に富んだ遊歩道が囲む。

Ⓣ03-5608-1111 Ⓐ1-12-10 Yokotuna, Sumida-ku Ⓞ9am-4:30pm daily

Heiseiteien
平成庭園

The sukiya tea-ceremony building overhanging the pond is beautiful.
池に張り出す数寄屋造りの建物が美しい。

Ⓣ03-3680-0777 Ⓐ3-2-1 Kitakasai, Edogawa-ku Ⓞ24hr. daily

Mukouzimahyakkaen
向島百花園

In this garden, created by Edo period literary man, seasonal flowers blossom.
江戸の文人が造った、四季の花が咲く庭。

Ⓣ03-3611-8705 Ⓐ3-18-3 Higashi-mukouzima, Sumida-ku Ⓞ9am-5pm daily Ⓕ¥150

KyuShibarikyu-onshiteien
旧芝離宮恩賜庭園

This garden of a daimyo lord from the early Edo period.
江戸初期の大名庭園。

Ⓣ03-3434-4029 Ⓐ1 Kaigan, Minato-ku Ⓞ9am-5pm daily Ⓕ¥150

高尾山
Takao-san
(Mt. Takao)

A treasure-trove of nature close to the city
都会近くの自然の宝庫

Standing at 599 meters, Mount Takao-san is located within the city of Hachioji in Western Tokyo. It can be easily climbed using a cable-car. Very popular as a getaway spot for enjoying nature close to the city, it was selected in 2007 as a Michelin 3-star tourist location. The great taste of natural foods such as sansai mountain vegetables and soba noodles is also a major attraction.

東京都西部、八王子市にある標高599mの山。ケーブルカーなどを利用して手軽に登ることができる。都心近郊にあって自然を感じられる行楽地として人気で、2007年にはミシュランの三つ星観光地にも選定された。そばや山菜など、自然の恵みを感じられる味覚も魅力。

Four seasons of scenery
四季の風景

A great view of Mt Fuji from the mountaintop observation deck
山頂の展望台から富士山を望む

City lights at night, seen from the beer garden that opens in summer
夏にオープンするビアガーデンからの夜景

Mountain cherry blossoms and violets bloom in spring
春には山桜やスミレなどが咲く

The approach to the summit
山頂へのアプローチ

Catch a cable car or a lift halfway up to the mountain. Both 470 yen each way.
山の中腹までケーブルカーとリフトが運行。どちらも片道470円。

Cable car
ケーブルカー

Lift
リフト

Takao-san Yakuouin Yukizi

高尾山薬王院有喜寺

This historic temple was constructed in the Nara period. Visiting the temple is said to bring good fortune.

奈良時代に建立された歴史ある寺院。参拝すると様々なご利益があると言われる。

Ⓣ042-661-1115

Many worshipers visit the Hon-do
多くの参拝客が訪れる本堂

A good-luck charm makes a nice souvenir
縁結びのお守りをおみやげに

Try shugyo (ascetic training) standing under a waterfall
滝に打たれる修行の体験もできる

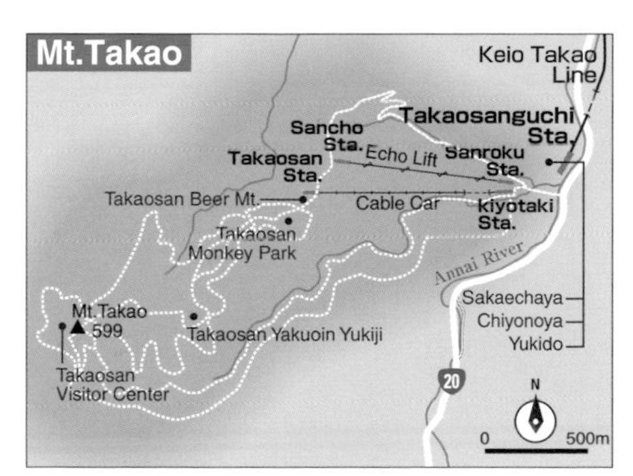

Takao-san Monkey Park

高尾山さる園

Around 40 nihonzaru monkeys roam freely inside the park.

園内には約40頭のニホンザルが放し飼いにされている。

Ⓣ042-661-2381
Ⓞ9:30am-4pm
Ⓒunsettled
Ⓕ¥400

Takao-san cuisine and souvenirs

高尾山グルメ&みやげ

Soba noodles.

そば

Watch professionals chopping noodles.

職人がそばを打つ様子も見られる。

Sakaechaya
Ⓣ042-661-0350
Ⓞ11am-7pm daily

Manju buns

まんじゅう

Filled with sweet red bean paste, the buns havc a delicate alcoholic fragrance.¥120

中は餡で、皮はほのかに酒の香りがする1個120円。

Chiyonoya The Head Store
Ⓣ042-661-4118
Ⓞ10am-5pm ⒸMon

Sembei crackers

せんべい

Maple-leaf shaped crackers are a favorite sou venir.¥504(15Pieces)

もみじ型せんべいは土産の定番15枚入り504円。

Youkido The Head Store
Ⓣ042-661-0048 Ⓞ9am-6pm ⒸTue

Revolving *kaiten* sushi bars

回転寿司

Simple, easy sushi for common folks

手軽な庶民の寿司

With its simple bill system, kaiten zushi (sushi) is a staple dining option for the Japanese. Just choose whatever sushi you like.

明朗会計の回転寿司は、日本人の外食の定番。好きなネタを食べたいだけどうぞ。

1

The price is determined by the color of the plate.
皿の色ごとに価格が決まっている

2

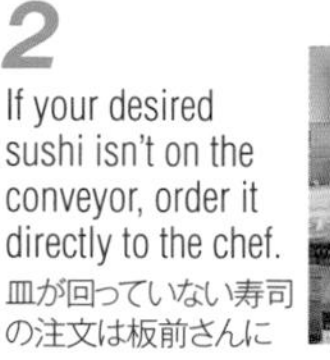

If your desired sushi isn't on the conveyor, order it directly to the chef.
皿が回っていない寿司の注文は板前さんに

3

Place powdered green tea in the cup, and pour your own hot water.
お茶はコップに粉末茶を入れ、自分でお湯を注ぐ

Some kaiten zushi guidelines

これが回転寿司

Welcome!
いらっしゃい！

Kakiya-sushi Harajuku
Ⓣ03-3423-1400
Ⓞ11am-11pm daily

Popular sushi toppings
人気の寿司ネタ

Sweet shrimp ¥150
甘えび

An unexpected Combination of tastes!
意外な味の組合せ

Scallop with hot & sweet sauce ¥330
甘辛スパイシーほたて

California roll ¥240
カリフォルニアロール

Vegetarian rolll ¥240
ベジタリアンロール

With seafood, freshness is paramount!
魚介類は鮮度が命！

Salmon ¥150
サーモン

Horse mackerel ¥240
あじ

It's OK even if you don't like raw fish!
生魚が苦手でもOK！

Conger eel ¥240
穴子

Omelet with sushi rice ¥150
玉子

Sushi rice stuffed in fried bean curd ¥60
柚子いなり

And then dessert
食後はデザートを

Ice cream with dark molasses & kinako soybean flour ¥190
黒蜜きな粉アイス

Daigaku-imo: glazed sweet potato ¥190
大学芋

MORE!
And many more!
Kaiten sushi bars
まだある! 回転寿司店

Tsukiji Honten
築地本店
Ⓣ03-3464-1178 Ⓐ24-8 Udagawacho, Shibuya-ku Ⓞ11am-11pm daily

Kaitenzushi UOKI
回転寿司 魚喜
Ⓣ03-5575-3555 ⒶArc Mori Bidg 3F, 1-12-32 Akasaka, Minato-ku Ⓞ11am-10pm Ⓒunsettled

Counter sushi bars
カウンター寿司

Watch skilled chefs at work.
板前さんの技に注目

If you want to find genuine sushi, go to a sushi bar with counter seating. The sushi is made right on the spot from the various items laid out before you.

本格的な寿司を食べたいなら、カウンター席のある寿司屋に行ってみよう。目の前に並ぶネタを、その場で握って食べさせてくれる。

1 Sushi items laid out in a glass case.
ネタはガラスケースの中

2 Written specials of the day.
本日のおすすめが書いてある

3 The chef prepares sushi.
寿司を握る板前さん

4 The sweet pickled ginger garnish gari is a staple.
生姜の甘酢漬け「ガリ」

5 First, wipe your hands with a moist towel.
最初におしぼりで手を拭こう

6 You don't have to use chopsticks! You can use your hands here.
箸を使わず手で食べてもよい

7 The sushi is served on unique geta plates.
寿司はゲタという皿に盛られる

Counter seating
これがカウンター席

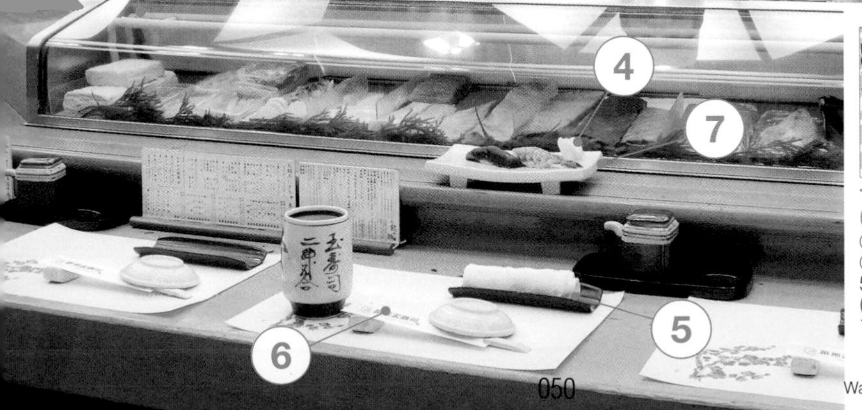

Tsukiji Tamazushi Ginza RABI
Ⓣ03-3574-9635
Ⓞ11:30am-5pm(6F), 5:30pm-2am(4/5F) (Sun, National Holiday 11:30am-10pm) daily

The ABC of sushi
寿司屋さんのいろは

A Various types of sushi
寿司のいろいろ

Chirashi ちらし
Various toppings laid out on top of seasoned rice ¥840
酢飯の上にさまざまなネタをトッピング

Nigiri 握り
Small seasoned rice balls topped with seafood
1piece ¥105~
小さく握った酢飯の上にネタがのる

Gunkan
軍艦
Seasoned rice balls wrapped in seaweed
1piece ¥105~
握りの酢飯を海苔でくるんだもの

Maki-zushi
巻き寿司
Seafood and seasoned rice rolled in seaweed using a sushi rolling mat
¥315~
巻き簀という道具を使い、ネタと酢飯を海苔で細長く巻く

Temaki 手巻き
Seafood and seasoned rice wrapped in a hand-sized piece of seaweed ¥210~
手のひらサイズの海苔で酢飯とネタを包む

B A few useful facts
知っておきたい豆知識

Tuna マグロ
Different parts of the same fish are known by different names. From the left, these sections of tuna are chu-toro, akami, and o-toro
同じ魚でも部位により呼び名が変わる。左からマグロの中トロ、赤身、大トロ

Soy Source 醤油
Apply just a little soy sauce to the topping of the sushi
醤油は寿司のネタの先に少しだけつける

Sake 酒
Japanese sake goes best with sushi. There are other side dishes such as sashimi
合わせる酒は日本酒がオススメ。刺身などの肴も揃う

C Sushi terminology
寿司用語集

Agari あがり	Green tea 茶
Oaiso おあいそ	The bill 会計
Shari シャリ	The seasoned rice part of sushi 寿司の酢飯の部分
Neta ネタ	The seafood topping part of sushi 寿司の上にのっている刺身
Murasaki むらさき	Soy sauce 醤油
Namida なみだ	Wasabi paste ワサビ
Gyoku ギョク	Fried egg 玉子焼き

MORE!

And many more!
Counter sushi bars
まだある! カウンター寿司

Sushi Hasegawa NIshiazabu
寿司 はせ川 西麻布店
Ⓣ03-5775-0510
ⒶKasumi Heights 2F 1-7-11 Nishi-Azabu, Minato-ku
Ⓞ6pm-3am ⒸSun

Midori Sohonten Shibuya
美登利総本店 渋谷店
Ⓣ03-5458-0002 ⒶMarkcity East 4F 1-12-3 Dougenzaka, Shibuya-ku Ⓞ11am-2:45pmLO, 5pm-9:45pmLO(Sat, Sun, National Holiday 11am-9pmLO) daily

Sukiyaki or shabushabu?

すき焼き？ それともしゃぶしゃぶ？

These are both popular meat dishes.

どちらも人気の肉料理

Sukiyaki has a stronger flavor, while shabushabu is milder.

濃い目の味のすき焼きと、
さっぱりとしたしゃぶしゃぶ。

Sukiyaki

すき焼き

A sweet, spicy dish of thin slices of beef and vegetables simmered with soy sauce and sugar.

薄切りの牛肉と野菜などの具材を、
醤油と砂糖で甘辛く煮た料理。

Flavored with a warishita soy sauce base
醤油ベースの「割下」で味付け

A shallow metal pan is used.
浅めの鉄鍋を使用

It also contains vegetables and tofu.
野菜や豆腐も入る

How to enjoy sukiyaki

すき焼きの食べ方

Japanese favorite!
日本人の好物！

1 Pour in the soy sauce base and cook the meat.
割下を入れて肉を焼く

2 Put in the other ingredients and simmer.
ほかの具を入れて煮る

3 Dip in raw egg and eat.
生卵につけて食べる

Asakusa Imahan Kokusaidori Honten

Ⓣ03-3841-1114
Ⓞ11:30am-8:30pmLO daily
Ⓕ¥6300~(for one)

Shabushabu

しゃぶしゃぶ

Swirl thin slices of meat around in boiling water, and then dip in sauce before eating.

沸騰した湯に薄切りの肉をくぐらせ、タレに付けて食べる。

In general, thinly sliced beef is served
ごく薄く切った牛肉を使用するのが特徴

The 2 basic types of sauce are sesame and ponzu (citrus sauce)
胡麻ダレとポン酢の2種類が基本

Include any seasonings you like, such as Welsh onion.
好みでネギなどの薬味を入れる

How to enjoy shabushabu

しゃぶしゃぶの食べ方

Two kinds of taste!
2種類の味！

1. Just immerse the meat in the boiling water.
肉は湯にくぐらせる程度で

2. Put in the vegetables, starting with those that take longest to cook.
野菜は煮えにくい物から入れる

3. Dip in your favorite sauce and enjoy!
好みのタレにつけて食べる

Kisoji Shinjuku Sanchome

Ⓣ03-3226-0667 Ⓞ11:30 am-3pm,5pm-10:30pm (Sat,Sun,National Holiday-10pm)daily Ⓕ¥4515～ (for one)

Japanese-style seating
お座敷
Stretch out your legs and relax.
足をくずしてくつろげる

Izakaya
居酒屋

Popular with young & old, men & women
老若男女が集う

Shoe cabinet
下駄箱
Shoes should be removed before using Japanese-style seating.
座敷に座る時には靴を脱ぐ

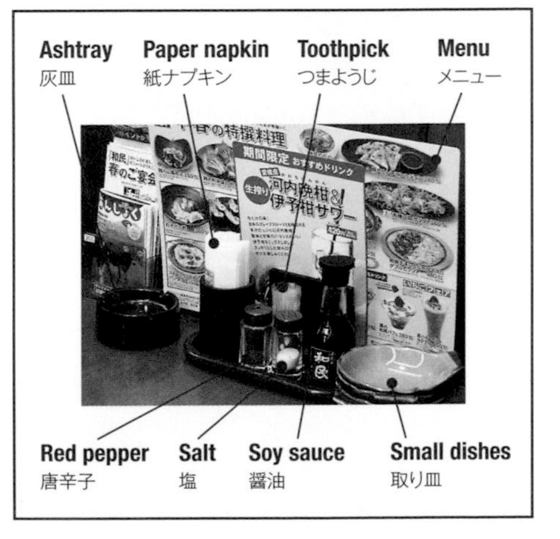

An izakaya is a place that serves alcohol and food to accompany it. Many of these are chain stores, with a diverse and inexpensive menu ranging from rice dishes through to desserts.

居酒屋とは酒とそれに合う料理を出す店。チェーン展開する店も多く、ご飯ものからデザートまで、安くて豊富なメニューが魅力。

Watami Ginza Sukiyabashi
Ⓣ03-5537-2695
Ⓞ5pm-3am (Fri,Sat-5am) daily

Drinks
ドリンク

Shochu ¥313~ 焼酎
Shochu can be made from various ingredients: potato, rice, grain, sugar, and more.
芋·米·麦·黒糖など原料はさまざま

Ume-shu plum wine ¥418~ 梅酒
A unique liqueur made from Japanese green ume plums
日本独自の青梅のリキュール

Sour ¥313~
サワー
Smooth and easy to drink, chu-hai sours are quite popular with women.
爽やかな飲み口で女性に人気

Draft beer ¥481~
中生
Medium-size draft beer
中サイズの生ビール

Food
フード

Kushi-yaki skewer assortment ¥628
串焼の盛合せ
Various parts of grilled chicken served on one plate
さまざまな部位の焼き鳥が一皿に

Eda-mame soy beans ¥313
枝豆
Steamed or boiled soy beans are perfect with beer.
茹でた枝豆は、ビールと相性抜群

Stir-fried udon noodles ¥418 焼うどん
Noodle or rice dishes are often eaten as a mop-up.
〆には麺類やご飯ものを

Warabi-mochi rice cake with vanilla ice cream ¥313
わらびもちとバニラアイス
A wide variety of Eastern and Western desserts is available
デザートも和洋充実している

Bonito sushi ¥418 カツオの寿司
Sushi is also reasonably priced.
寿司もリーズナブル

Yose dohu (tofu bean curd) ¥523 寄せ豆腐
Healthy tofu is always on the izakaya menu
ヘルシーな豆腐も居酒屋の定番

MORE!

And many more! **Izakaya**
まだある! 居酒屋

Shoya Shibuya
庄や 渋谷店
Ⓣ03-3496-4811 ⒶB1F, 24-10 Udagawacho, Shibuya-ku
Ⓞ5pm-4am daily

Shirokiya Hibiya Ekimae
白木屋 日比谷駅前店
Ⓣ03-3501-5488
ⒶDaini Hibiya Bldg 5F, 1-6-1 Yurakucho, Chiyoda-ku
Ⓞ5pm-5am(Sun,National Holiday-12am) daily

Mega appliance stores

大型家電量販店

Huge sales all year round!

年中大売り出し!

An 8-floor chain store selling household appliances, computers, cameras, sports gears, toys – they have everything from alcohol to designer fashion goods, and it's all cheap.

8フロアからなる家電量販チェーン店。パソコンにカメラはもちろん、スポーツ用品におもちゃ、お酒にブランド品まで格安で販売。

Bic Camera Yurakucho Honkan
Ⓣ03-5221-1111
Ⓞ10am-10pm daily

Games ゲーム
You can try out new games.
新作ゲームも試せます

They even sell alcohol.
お酒も販売
They won't be beaten on their range, even by specialty stores.
専門店にも負けない品揃え

Pedometer
万歩計

Attach it to yourself and it displays how many steps you've taken.

身に付けておくと歩いた歩数を表示

A toilet seat with a washing function
温水洗浄便座

A multifunction toilet seat with a seat-warming function

お尻温め機能も付いた多機能便座

※価格は変更の場合あり

Lint remover
毛玉取り器

For removing pilling, fluff, and lint from clothing

服に付いた毛玉を除去

These handy appliances are quintessentially Japanese.

日本ならではのお役立ち家電

Footbath フットバス

Pour hot water in and enjoy a foot massage.

お湯を入れて足をマッサージ♪

Hotplate with takoyaki maker
たこ焼き器付きホットプレート

Of course, you can use it for things other than takoyaki (octopus balls).

プレートを付け替えればたこ焼き以外にも使えます

Rice cooker
炊飯器

This indispensable Japanese household item cooks rice automatically.

自動で米が炊ける日本家庭の必需品

Whatever you need, leave it to us!

どんな家電もおまかせください!

Massage machine demonstration
マッサージ機体験

Is this where hard-working businessmen come to relax?

サラリーマンの憩いの場?

Price tags
値札

Red-on-yellow lettering is common.

黄色に赤が基本です

Point cards ポイントカード

Use your saved points for next shopping. 1point is ¥1.

貯まったポイントは、1ポイント1円で次の買物で使用できる

MORE!

And many more!
Mega appliance stores
まだある! 大型家電量販店

Yodobashi Camera Multimedia Akiba
ヨドバシカメラ マルチメディア Akiba
Ⓣ03-5209-1010
Ⓐ1-1 Kanda-Hanaokacho, chiyoda-ku Ⓞ9:30am-10pm daily

YAMADADenki LABI Ikebukuro
ヤマダ電機 LABI 池袋
Ⓣ03-5958-7770
Ⓐ1-41-1 Higashi-Ikebukuro, Toshima-ku Ⓞ10am-10pm daily

Discount stores

ディスカウントストア

An exposition of Japanese culture

ジャパンカルチャーの見本市

Don Quijote

ドン・キホーテ

Thousands of items on display: knick-knacks, foodstuffs, designer goods, cosmetics, appliances, and more. A veritable discount palace!

雑貨や食料品、ブランド品、コスメや家電など数万点が並ぶ。まさに「激安の殿堂」。

Samurai wig
¥1480 侍カツラ
Transform instantly into a samurai.
一瞬でサムライに変身

Bakkanto sweating-bath powder
¥248
爆汗湯
This bath powder is effective (!?) for burning body fat.
脂肪燃焼効果のある(!?)入浴剤

Millionaire trunks
¥1480 成金トランクス
Printed with Japanese banknote designs
日本のお札がプリントされている

Yves Saint Laurent Baby Doll Sweet Love ¥1980
イヴ・サンローラン・ベビードール スウィートラブ
A sweet, fragrant eau de cologne
甘〜い香りの香水

Nose-hair trimmer
¥980 鼻毛カッター
Trim your nose-hair before a big date.
デートの前は鼻毛を手入れ

Kewpie ornament
¥498
キューピー根付
An Edo-period plaything. Ideal as a cell-phone strap
江戸玩具調。携帯ストラップに

BVLGARI BLV for Ladies
¥2980 ブルガリ ブルー(レディース)
Everyday cheap prices for brand name fragrances!
ブランド香水も毎日激安!

Don Quijote Roppongi
Ⓣ03-5786-0811
Ⓞ24hr. daily

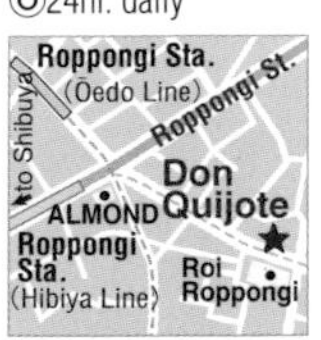

One coin shops
100円ショップダイソー

All kinds of products at a flat price of 100 yen (105 yen with tax). Great for souvenirs of Japan. See what you can find.

あらゆるジャンルの商品が100円均一(税込105円)。日本みやげのオススメ、探してみました。

NB:Some items in the store may be priced higher than 100 yen, and some items may not be currently in stock.
※店内には100円以外の商品もある。在庫がない場合もあり

Daruma
だるま
Daruma ornaments are said to bring good luck.
幸運を呼ぶといわれる置物

Marbles
ビー玉
Made of glass, these toys have been popular since ancient times.
ガラスでできた昔ながらの玩具

Paper balloon
紙風船
This balloon is made from Japanese washi paper.
和紙を張り合わせた風船

Tokuri flask
徳利
Essential for serving Japanese sake
日本酒には徳利が必需品

Shishi-odoshi bamboo deer-scarer & stone lantern
ししおどしと石灯籠
Create a miniature Japanese garden at home.
自宅にミニチュア日本庭園を

Pouch
ポーチ
With attractive indigo blue pattern
藍染め風の柄がポイント

The Harajuku Daiso
Ⓣ0824-200-100 (Main office)
Ⓞ10am-9pm daily

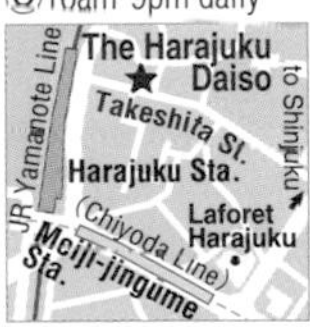

Souvenirs of Japan
日本みやげ

The Japanese taste is spreading all over the world.
世界に広がる"和"テイスト

Kanji lettering & Japanese patterns
漢字&和柄

Guaranteed to garner attention. The most popular items.
目立つこと請け合い。一番人気のアイテム。

This Japanese-patterned bag goes very well with regular outfits too. ¥2300
普段着にも合う和柄のバッグ

Ichiban (Number 1) T-shirt ¥1000
「一番」(ナンバーワン) Tシャツ

The image of Astro Boy changes depending on your viewing angle ¥3900
角度によって「アトム」の絵が変わる

Wrap it around your head when you need to make an all-out effort! ¥500
気合いを入れたいときに頭に巻こう

Manage your hair with an attractive hair clip. ¥1200
まとめ髪のポイントに。髪どめ

For a coordinated accent. ¥1900～
コーディネートのアクセントに

Maneki neko
招き猫

This cat ornament brings good fortune. The right hand is said to invite wealth, while the left beckons people closer.
幸運を呼ぶ猫の置物。右足で金運、左足で人を招くといわれる。

With both hands raised, you receive twice as much luck! ¥800
両手を挙げて幸運も2倍!

With a roll of banknotes attached, your luck is even better. ¥1680
札束付きで縁起がいい

Gold! what a gorgeous! ¥2900
金色! なんてゴージャスな!

Japanese knick-knacks
和雑貨

These small everyday items make a fine memento of your trip.
毎日使える雑貨を、旅の思い出とともに。

Metal-chased plate depicting rear view of maiko ¥1600
舞妓の後ろ姿が艶やかな彫金絵皿

Sushi design and name-labeled mug ¥840
寿司の絵と名前入りのマグカップ

Kokeshi make ideal souvenirs to give young girls. ¥1800
「こけし」は女の子へのおみやげに

Tapestry with Japanese map design ¥740
日本地図柄のタペストリー

Ukiyo-e design chopsticks: use them as a pair. ¥530
ペアで使いたい浮世絵箸

Wakuwaku Tarono Yorozubako
Ⓣ03-3253-9779
Ⓞ11am-8pm(Sat-7pm,Sun,National Holiday-6pm) daily

Foreign currency exchange is also available
外貨両替もできる

Character merchandise
キャラクターグッズ

Popular characters loved all over the world
世界中で愛される人気者

Hello Kitty
ハローキティ

This white kitten is "Hello Kitty," born in 1974. Note the trademark ribbon on her ear. Her favorite is apple pies.

1974年生まれの白い子猫のキャラクター、「キティちゃん」。耳のリボンが目印。好物はアップルパイ！

The ever-popular soft toy (M) ¥3675
定番人気のぬいぐるみ

Toothbrush set with cup ¥693
コップも付いた歯磨きセット

Pouch shaped like Kitty's face ¥1575
キティの顔型ポーチ

Sanrio Shop Shinjuku Gift Gate Elegant
Ⓣ03-3354-3640 Ⓞ10am-9pm (Sat, Sun, National Holiday -8pm) Ⓒunsettled

Pokémon (Pockét Monsters)
ポケモン(ポケットモンスター)

These characters first appeared in video games. The hugely popular animated series is now broadcast in 70 countries and regions.

ゲームソフトから誕生したポケモン。アニメはこれまで世界70の国と地域で放送された大人気番組。

"Hikozaru (Chimchar)" soft toy ¥950
「ヒコザル」のぬいぐるみ

"Pochama (Piplup)" soft toy ¥950
「ポッチャマ」のぬいぐるみ

The ever-popular "Pikachu" soft toy ¥950
人気の「ピカチュウ」のぬいぐるみ

Pokémon Center TOKYO
Ⓣ03-6430-7733 Ⓞ11am-8pm (Sat, Sun, National Holiday 10am-7pm) Ⓒunsettled

STUDIO GHIBLI merchandise

スタジオジブリ キャラクターグッズ

Characters from the Academy Award-winning "Spirited Away" and "My Neighbor Totoro"

アカデミー賞受賞「千と千尋の神隠し」などの
スタジオジブリキャラクターグッズが勢揃い。

"Large Totoro" soft toy (S)
¥1680
「となりのトトロ」ぬいぐるみ
大トトロ 濃グレー（S）笑い

Magnet depicting Jiji from "Kiki's Delivery Service" ¥924
「魔女の宅急便」ジジくたくたマグネット
©1989 角野栄子・二馬力・GN

Music-box from "My Neighbor Totoro"
¥3990
「となりのトトロ」オルゴール 花摘み ネコバス
©二馬力

Key holder with the Kaonashi from "Spirited Away" ¥525
「千と千尋の神隠し」根付コレクション カオナシ

Donguri Kyowakoku Venus Fort Family
Ⓣ03-3570-5091
Ⓞ11am-8pm
Ⓒunsettled

More popular characters

まだある人気キャラクター

Thc "Doraemon and Anpanman" animated series are loved by children around the world.

世界の子供たちに大人気のアニメ、
「ドラえもん」に「アンパンマン」

Anpanman" face towel
¥630
「アンパンマン」の顔型フェイスタオル
©やなせたかし／フレーベル館・TMS・NTV

"Doraemon" puppet cushion
¥1344
「ドラえもん」のパペット兼クッション
©Fujiko-Pro, Shogakukan,TV-Asahi, Shin-ei, and ADK

KIDDY LAND HARAJUKU
Ⓣ03-3409-3431
Ⓞ10am-9pm
Ⓒunsettled

Kabuki
歌舞伎

The stage upon which only men may perform
男性だけが上がることを許された舞台

Kabuki is a traditional Japanese art form that commenced in the early Edo period, said to comprise a body of roughly 400 works. Kabuki is characteristically performed only by male actors who wear unique make-up. Performances are held almost daily at the Kabuki-za Theater, and tickets can be purchased at the ticket counter of the Kabuki-za Theater, etc.

江戸時代初期に始まった日本の伝統芸能。作品数は約400本といわれ、独特の化粧をした男性俳優のみで演じられるのが特徴。公演はほぼ毎日歌舞伎座で行われており、チケットは歌舞伎座のチケット売り場などで購入できる。

Kabuki-za
Ⓣ03-3541-3131
ⒻAbout ¥1000(one act)

Kabuki terminology
歌舞伎用語

Kurogo
黒衣
A stage attendant dressed in black who assists the costumed actors
黒い衣装をまとい役者の手伝いをする人

Makunouchi bento (interval lunch)
幕の内弁当
These can be ordered before the show or during intermission.
開幕前や幕間に頼むことができる

Kojo (verbal message)
口上
A custom where the actors assemble onstage and greet the assembled patrons
役者が舞台の上にズラリと並び、客席に向かって挨拶すること

Joshikimaku (regularly-used curtain)
定式幕
The 3-colored curtain that hangs onstage. At the Kabuki-za, it is black, orange, and green (left to right)
舞台にかかる三色縦縞の幕。歌舞伎座は左から黒、オレンジ、緑

Hanamichi (lit. flower path)
花道
A runway-like projection from the stage, used by actors making entrances and exits
役者が舞台へ出入りする際に使う通路状の部分

Kumadori make-up
隈取
A style of make-up in which red, blue, and black lines are drawn on the limbs over a white background
白塗りした手足に赤·青·黒の絵具で線を描く化粧法

Mie
見得
A unique performance technique where actors pause and hold a pose for important scenes
重要な場面などで静止してポーズを取る独特の演出

The kabuki stage
歌舞伎の舞台
Shimote
下手
The right-hand side of the stage
舞台右側
Odogu (large props)
大道具
One highlight is the elaborate set.
見どころのひとつは豪華なセット
Kamite
上手
The left-hand side of the stage
舞台左側
LEISURE
遊ぶ
Onnagata
女方
Female roles played by men. Watch their mannerisms closely.
男性によって演じられる。仕草にも注目
Honbutai
(The main stage)
本舞台
The performers
登場人物
Make-up
化粧
Compelling and remarkable Kumadori make-up
迫力満点の隈取
Wig
かつら
These vary depending on the type of role.
役柄ごとに使い分ける
Kodogu (props)
小道具
Used for direct expression of a role's personality
役の性格を端的に表す
Costumes
衣裳
Watch the skilled use of these elaborate kimonos.
豪華な着物の着こなしに注目
Hints when going to see Kabuki
鑑賞のヒント
Earphones with English commentary available (charge applies)
英語の解説が聞けるイヤホンガイド（有料）
English programs available (¥500)
英語版プログラムは500円
Some flexible seats are available for viewing only one act from the program (only by same-day purchase)
一幕だけを鑑賞できる一幕見席もある(当日券のみ)

写真提供・松竹株式会社

Sumo
相撲

A martial tradition with ancient history
古来より伝わる武道

Loincloth-clad wrestlers within a circular clay ring, locked in a struggle for victory; this is sumo, the national sport of Japan. A wrestler loses if he moves outside the ring, or if any part of his body apart from the soles of his feet touches the ground.
　まわし姿の力士が丸い土俵の中で組み合い、勝ち負けを競う日本の国技。土俵の外に出るか、足の裏以外が地面に付いたら負けとなる。

Ryogoku Kokugikan
Ⓣ03-3623-5111 (Nihon Sumo Kyokai)
Ⓕ¥2100~

Inside the venue
場内の様子

① **Man'in-o-rei (A greeting thanking for sellout crowd)** 満員御礼
The curtain is lowered whenever the venue is full.
場内が満席になると下ろされる幕

② **Hanging roof** 吊り屋根
This roof is 10m square and 8.6m tall.
縦横各10m、高さ8.6mの大きな屋根

③ **Mizuhiki maku water curtain** 水引幕
This purple curtain symbolizes water.
水を表す紫色の幕

④ **Dohyo (the ring)** 土俵
4.55 meters in diameter, it takes around 3 days to create.
直径4.55m。約3日間かけて作る

A sumo wrestler
これが力士だ

Oicho hairstyle
大銀杏
Only Sekitori ranking wrestlers may wear their hair in this style
関取力士のみが結える髪型

Kessho-mawashi
化粧まわし
A brilliant garment used only when entering the ring
土俵入専用の華やかなまわし

Mawashi
まわし
A type of loincloth worn when performing sumo
相撲を取る際に着けるふんどしの一種

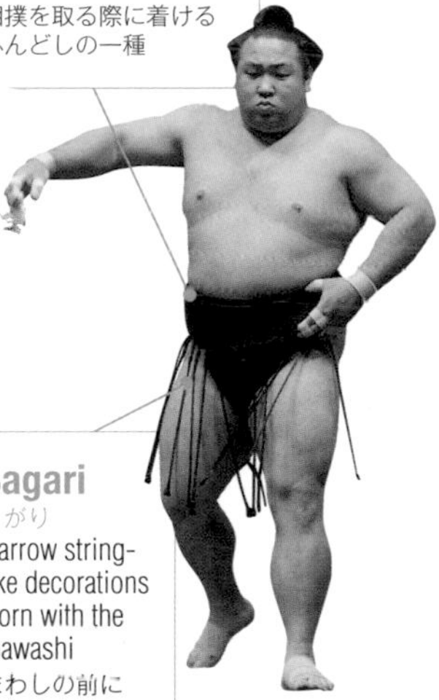

Gyoji (referee)
行司
Wearing unique clothing and carrying a Gunbai fan, he judges the sumo match
独特の衣装で軍配を持つ、相撲の審判

Sagari
さがり
Narrow string-like decorations worn with the mawashi
まわしの前に挟むひも状の飾り

⑤ **Shibusa (four tassels)** 四房
4 colored tassels are suspended from the corners of the hanging roof.
吊り屋根の四隅を飾る4色の房

⑥ **Masu seating** マス席
Partitioned seating on the 1st floor to view the action with a few people.
数人で観戦するよう仕切られた1階の席

⑦ **Chair seating** イス席
These seats are located on the 2nd floor section.
2階部分に設けられた席

⑧ **Tamari ringside seating** タマリ席
The closest seats to the ring. Also known as the "suna-kaburi (sand-sprinkled seats)".
土俵に一番近い席。別名「砂かぶり」

Sumo merchandise on sale at the Kokugikan sumo stadium
国技館で買える相撲グッズ

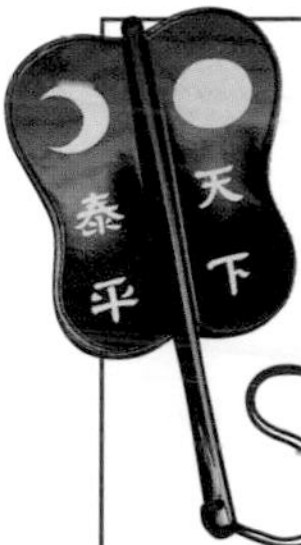

Toy gunbai fan ¥750
おもちゃの軍配

Small fan with popular wrestlers ¥450
人気力士の豆うちわ

Tea cup with sumo designs 2 for ¥1050
相撲が描かれた湯呑み

Sento bathhouse

銭湯

If you've come this far, you're a connoisseur of Japan.

ここまでくれば日本通

The public bathhouse of bygone days is still a popular meeting place for those living downtown. Enjoy the retro atmosphere!

昔ながらの公衆浴場は、今も下町の人々の社交場。レトロな空間を満喫しよう！

Tsurunoyu
Ⓣ03-3821-2514
Ⓞ4pm-12am
ⒸSat Ⓕ¥430
Bring a towel and soap etc.
※タオル・石けんなどは持参のこと

This is the sento.

これが銭湯だ

The characteristic appearance resembles a temple or shrine building.
寺社建築のような外観が特徴的

The change room is for undressing. Place valuables inside a locker.
服を脱ぐ脱衣所。貴重品はロッカーへ

Place your clothes in the basket and head for the bath
脱いだ衣類はかごに入れ浴室へ

The tall chimney is symbolic. There is the one not used either now.
高い煙突がシンボル。今は使われていないものもある

Stepping out of the bath

湯上がりには

Well-chilled milk is perfect after a bath! ¥110
よく冷えた牛乳が最高。¥110

You can cool off in the inner garden too.
中庭に出て涼むのもいい

A standard item: the free massage chair
定番のマッサージチェアは無料

The main bathing room
浴室

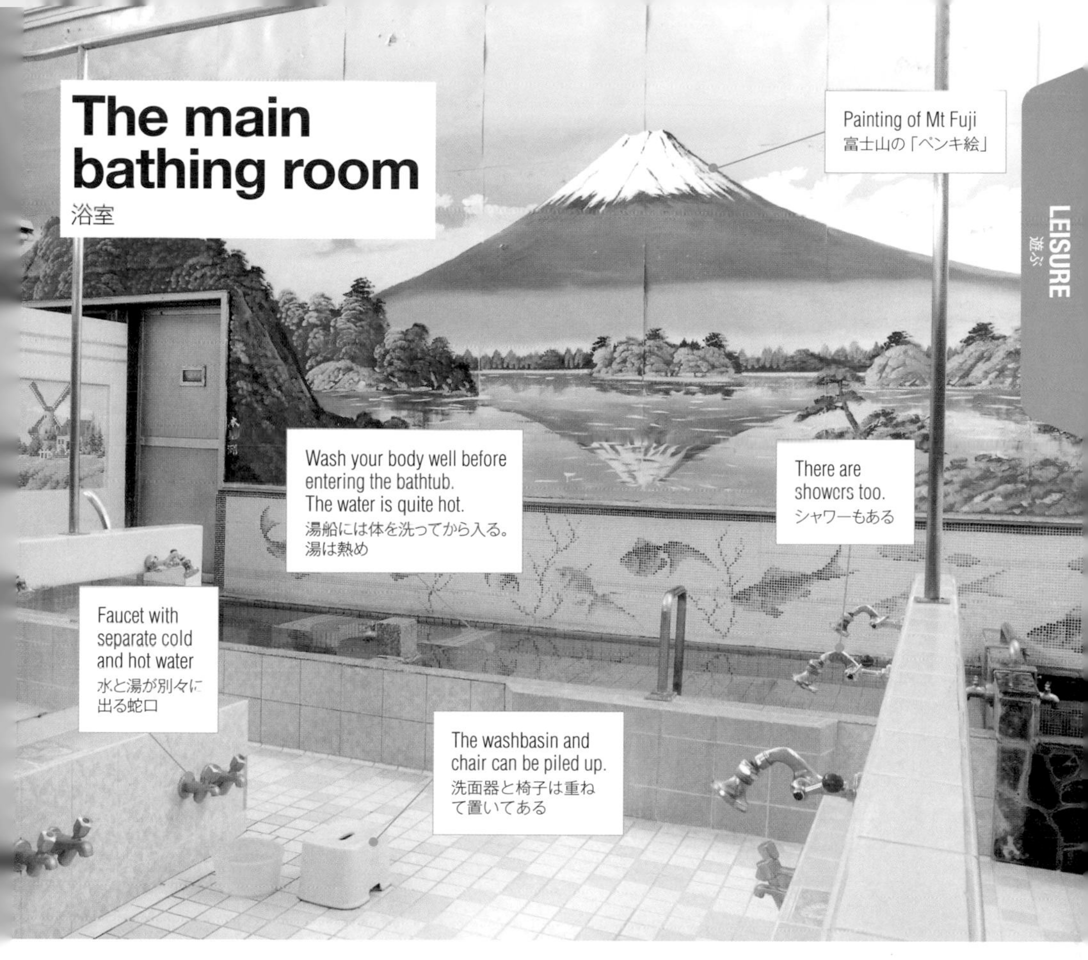

An evolution in sento 進化した銭湯

Super sento! スーパー銭湯

Oedo Onsen Monogatari
大江戸温泉物語

Full marks for Edo-period charm. The outdoor bath and footbath facilities are also available.
江戸情緒満点。露天風呂に足湯もある。

Ⓣ03-5500-1126
Ⓞ11am-9am daily
Ⓕ¥2827

The largest spa facility in Japan, it has an amusement park next door.
国内最大級のスパ施設。隣には遊園地もある。

Ⓣ03-5800-9999
Ⓞ11am-9am daily Ⓕ¥2565

Maiko
舞妓

Transform into a maiko in Tokyo.
東京で舞妓になれます

A geiko sings and dances to entertain at formal functions. Apprentice geisya, still studying, are known as maiko.

　舞踏や唄などで宴席を盛りあげる芸者。その見習いとして勉強中の女性を舞妓という。

COCOMO
Ⓣ03-3847-0763
Ⓞ9am-8pm daily
Ⓕ¥18800~
(including 3 pictures)
＊Reservation required

Undergo your own maiko transformation!
舞妓に変身体験

Maiko
これが舞妓さん

Kanzashi
かんざし
Showy hair ornament with hanging section
下がりのついた派手な髪飾り

Ware-shinobu
割れしのぶ
The hairstyle of young maiko. The hair is set with her own hair.
若い舞妓の髪型。地髪で結う

Japanese handbag
和装バッグ
Japanese patterned bags match the kimono
着物に合わせる和柄のバッグ

Obi belt
帯
The belt, known as darari-obi, is over 5 meters in length.
「だらりの帯」と呼ばれる長さ5m以上の帯

Furisode
振袖
The long split sleeve is characteristic.
袖の「袂」が長いのが特徴

Naga-juban (long undergarment)
長襦袢
This juban is worn beneath the kimono.
着物の下に着るのが「襦袢」

Tabi socks
足袋
White is the basic color.
足袋は白が基本

Pokkuri sandals
ぽっくり
Maiko wears thick-soled wooden sandals.
厚底の下駄を履く

Kyoto dialect as used by maiko-san
舞妓さんの使う京ことば

okoshiyasu (おこしやす)
➲Welcome いらっしゃいませ

akimahen (あきまへん)
➲That's no good. 駄目です

okini (おおきに)
➲Thank you. ありがとうございます

kannine (かんにんえ)
➲Sorry. ごめんなさい

okibariyasu (おきばりやす)
➲Good luck. / Work hard.
頑張ってください

MORE!
And many more!
Maiko transformations
まだある! 舞妓体験

Henshin Studio Mon KATSURA
変身スタジオ モン かつら
Ⓣ03-3470-0027 Ⓐ4-28-4 Jingu-mae, Shibuya-ku Ⓞ10am-6pm daily Ⓕ¥18000～(including 3 pictures)

Showroom

ショールーム

Experience the latest Japanese technology.

日本の最新技術を体感

Japanese advanced technology leads the world! Glimpse the future at this showroom with technologies from all the leading companies.

日本のハイテク技術は世界の最先端！　各企業の技術の粋を集結させたショールームで未来を覗こう。

You can test drive hybrid vehicles designed for children on the indoor course.
室内コースでは子供向けのハイブリッドカートの試乗も

TOYOTA MEGA WEB

メガウェブ

An exhibition of the latest Toyota cars.
You can test drive them around the course.
There are also shopping and restaurant facilities.
最新のトヨタ車を展示。コースでは試乗もできる。
カフェレストランやショップも併設。

Toyota's advanced motor sports machines such as F1 cars are also shown here.
F1などトヨタが参戦するモータースポーツのマシンも展示

to Shinbashi
DECKS Tokyo Beach
Yurikamome
Rinkai Line
Tokyo Teleport Sta.
TOYOTA MEGA WEB
Omi Sta.

TOYOTA MEGA WEB
Ⓣ03-3599-0808
Ⓞ11am-9pm
Ⓒunsettled

This very popular spot has all the latest models on display.
最新モデルが並ぶコーナーは大人気

Ginza Sony Showroom

銀座ソニーショールーム

Here you can find displays, demonstrations, and explanation for new products prior to commercial release.

発売前の新商品の展示や体験、使い方の説明も行っている。

With the latest high-vision technology, the images and sound are overwhelming.

最新鋭のハイビジョンで、迫力の映像とサウンドを

Here you can customize your VAIO, a popular PC series.

人気のPC「VAIO」がカスタマイズできるコーナーも

Ginza Sony Showroom
Ⓣ03-3573-2563
Ⓞ11am-7pm daily

INAX GINZA

INAX GINZA

There are all kinds of INAX tiles, and presenting a huge range of appliances.

INAXの全種類のタイルと選りすぐった住宅設備機器に出合える。

There are many toilets here of sophisticated design.

洗練されたデザインのトイレが並ぶ

The first floor, completely covered in tiles, has a neo-futuristic feeling.

一面タイル貼りの1階フロアは、近未来的な印象

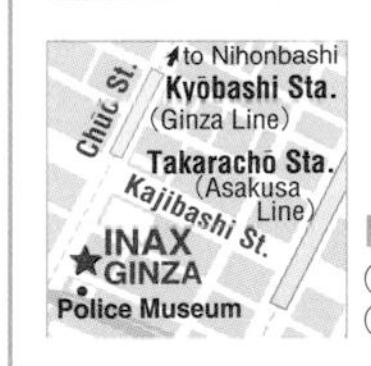

INAX GINZA
Ⓣ03-5250-6560 Ⓞ10am-6pm
ⒸSun,National Holiday

Panasonic Center TOKYO

パナソニックセンター東京

Apart from the latest products, there is also a wide range of exhibitions and opportunities to learn about the environment, science, and mathematics.

最新製品のほか、環境や理数学習の体験型展示まで幅広い。

Flat screen TVs on display, from 15V to 103V models

15V型～103V型までの薄型テレビが一同に

Kokusai Tenjijyo Sta.
Ariake Sta.
Rinkai Line
Yurikamome
Tokyo Bay Ariake Washington Hotel
Panasonic Center TOKYO

Panasonic Center TOKYO
Ⓣ03-3599-2600 Ⓞ10am-6pm ⒸMon

Gaming spots
プレイスポット

Just be careful not to enjoy yourself too much!
はまりすぎに注意！

Not just for kids! These areas are full of high-tech devices for grown adults to immerse themselves in.

たかが遊びと侮るなかれ。大人を熱中させるハイテク機器が満載だ。

©SEGA

Game centers
ゲームセンター

Enjoy the latest games for around 200 yen per play. You can win free prizes too!

1プレイ200円ほどで楽しめる最新ゲームが揃う。景品が獲れる場合も。

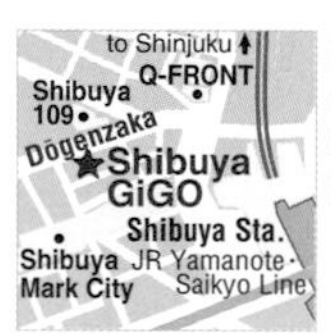

Shibuya GiGO
Ⓣ03-5458-2201
Ⓞ10pm-0am (Fri,Sat-1am) daily

Taiko no Tatsujin (Taiko: Drum Master)
太鼓の達人

Compete to see how accurately you can beat the drum in time with the music.
演奏曲に合わせて、いかに正確に太鼓を叩けるかを競う。

The prizes you fish out fall in here.
釣った商品はここに落ちてくる

UFO Catcher
UFOキャッチャー

Operate the crane and fish out all sorts of prizes!
クレーンを操作して、さまざまな景品を釣り上げよう！

Shooting games
シューティングゲーム

Grab a weapon and fight off ever-advancing enemies!
次々に迫り来る敵に、武器を取って立ち向かえ！

Pachinko

パチンコ

A Japanese-created game in which you move balls through a machine like pinball. Ages 18 and over.

ピンボールのように台に玉を転がす、日本生まれのゲーム。
18歳以上で遊技可能。

How to play Pachinko

どうやって遊ぶの？

1 Acquire some pachinko balls.
玉を借りる
You may have to buy a card first, or insert cash directly.
カードを買う場合と現金を直接入れる場合がある

2 Choose a machine.
台を選ぶ
Choose an empty seat.
人が座っていない台を選ぼう

3 Strike the balls.
玉を打つ
Adjust strike strength using the handle
ハンドルで玉の強さを調節

4 Big win! (Jackpot!)
大当たり!（フィーバー!）
Line up 3 of the same pattern to receive extra balls.
3つ同じ図柄が揃うと玉が増える

5 Exchange for prizes.
景品交換
You can exchange for prizes such as candies.
菓子などの景品と交換できる

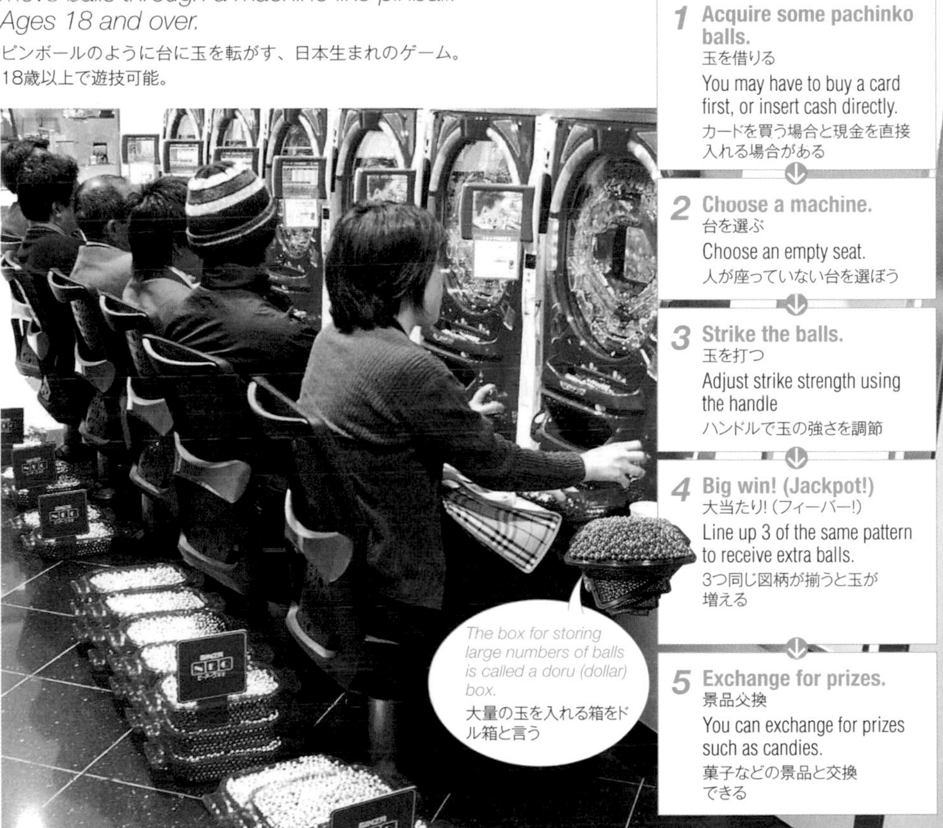

Pachinko machine

パチンコ台

Ryokan

旅館

Curious to sleep on tatami mats?

畳の上で寝てみたい?

If you want to stay in a Japanese environment, we recommend a ryokan inn. Many ryokan cater for foreign guests, and some have English-speaking staff.

和室に泊まりたいなら旅館がオススメ。外国人にも泊まりやすく、英語対応可能なところもある。

1 Tatami matting 畳
Traditional flooring material made from plant stalks
植物の茎で作る伝統的な床材

2 futon 布団
A futon set includes upper and lower futon quilts
掛布団と敷布団がセット

3 yukata 浴衣
A gown-like robe to wear in your room
ガウンのような部屋着

4 shoji 障子
Shoji screens are usually made from paper: be careful not to rip them!
紙なので破らないよう注意

Rooms

客室

5 zataku 座卓
This is where you sit to drink tea.
お茶を飲むときはここで

6 zabuton 座布団
Use this cushion when you sit.
座るときはこの上に

7 tokonoma 床の間
A hanging scroll usually decorates this raised floor section.
床が高くなった部分で、掛け軸などが飾られる

These services are available.

こんなサービスがあります

Postcards and other souvenirs on sale
ハガキなどのみやげも販売

English-language newspapers are available.
英字新聞もある

There are also many English-language tourist brochures.
英語の観光パンフレットも豊富

Free Internet use
無料でインターネットが使える

MORE

And many more!
Ryokan inns
まだある! 旅館

Hotel Edoya
ホテル江戸屋
Ⓣ03-3833-8751
Ⓐ3-20-3 Yushima,Bunkyo-ku
Ⓕ¥5890~(Room Rates for 1 person), ¥8540~(for 2 persons) on Sunday

Sukeroku No Yado SADACHIYO
助六の宿 貞千代
Ⓣ03-3842-6431
Ⓐ2-20-1 Asakusa,Taito-ku
Ⓕ¥14000~(Room Rates for 1 person), ¥19500~(for 2 persons)

Bathroom

浴室

Wash your body in the shower before entering.
シャワーで体を流してから入る

Don't place your towel in the water.
タオルをお湯につけない

Clean your body outside the bathtub.
体は浴槽の外で洗う

Don't pull out the plug when leaving.
出るときに詮は抜かない

Sawanoya Ryokan
Ⓣ03-3822-2251
Ⓕ¥5040~ (Room Rates for 1 person), ¥9450~ (for 2 persons)

Various hotels
ホテルいろいろ

The optimum stay for your budget
予算に応じた快適ステイ

There is great diversity in hotels from pricing through to systems, as well as some types exclusive to Japan.

値段からシステムまでさまざま。日本独自の形態のものも。

Naturally, the pool and jacuzzi are deluxe models.
プールやジャグジーも豪華版

High-end hotels
高級ホテル

All the world's leading hotels are represented in Tokyo. Luxurious spaces and attention to service remove you from everyday concerns.

世界の一流ホテルが集まる街、東京。ラグジュアリーな空間ときめ細かいサービスが非日常へと誘う。

The corridor library boasts 2000 books.
廊下には2000冊の蔵書を誇るライブラリーが

Brecthtaking views from guest room located on the 42nd floor or above.
42階以上の高層階にある客室は眺望抜群

PARK HYATT TOKYO
Ⓣ03-5322-1234
Ⓕ¥68200~
(Room Rates for 2 persons)

Business hotels

ビジネスホテル

Some rooms have washing machines, dryers, mini-kitchen, enabling a longer-term stay

洗濯機や乾燥機、ミニキッチンなどが付く部屋もあり、長期滞在も可能。

Tokyu Stay Yotsuya
Ⓣ03-3354-0109
Ⓕ¥9400~ (Room Rates for 1 person)

Single rooms are full of facilities packed into a compact space.
充実の設備がコンパクトにまとまったシングルルーム

The mini-kitchen has a microwave, electric stovetop, and refrigerator.
ミニキッチンには電子レンジと電気コンロ、冷蔵庫が

Unit bathroom containing towels, shampoo, etc.
タオルやシャンプーなどが揃うユニットバス

Capsule hotel

カプセルホテル

Offering a simple capsule-style bed with light, television, and so on, most capsule hotels are exclusively for men. Many boast a sauna and large bath.

照明やテレビなどが付いたカプセル状の簡易ベッドで、男性専用の場合が多い。サウナや大浴場があるところも。

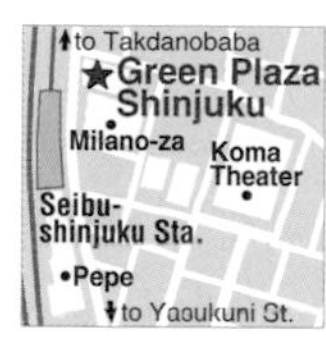

Green Plaza Shinjuku
Ⓣ03-3207-4923
Ⓕ¥4300~ (Room Rates for 1 person)

The large bathroom also boasts an outdoor bath.
大浴場には露天風呂

Sauna using Himalayan rock salt
ヒマラヤ岩塩を使ったサウナ

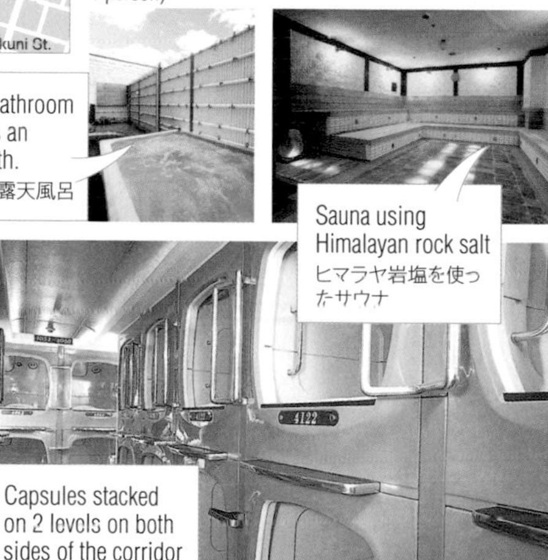

Capsules stacked on 2 levels on both sides of the corridor
通路の両側に2段に積まれた「カプセル」が並ぶ

Love hotels

ラブホテル

Accommodation facilities for lovers, these offer a diverse range of room designs depending on the hotel. Most offer check-in in the middle of the night, and room prices are often 10,000 yen or less.

恋人のための宿泊施設で、ホテルによって部屋にはさまざまな趣向が凝らされている。宿泊受付は夜遅くからの場合が多いが、料金はおおむね1万円以下。

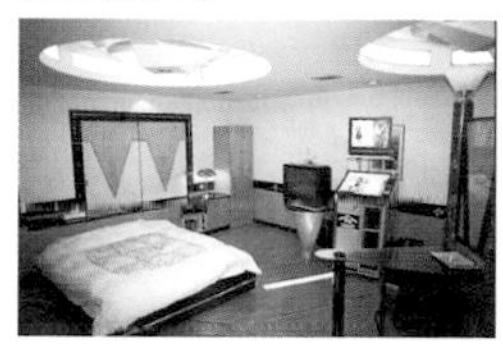

*Actual rooms may vary from photograph
※写真はイメージです

Tokyo sightseeing in a day
1日でめぐる東京

Hato Bus tour
はとバスツアー

If your stay in Tokyo is brief, catch the essential sights via a bus tour.
東京滞在が短いなら、定番スポットを回るバスツアーがオススメ。

The guide, Shibata-san
ガイドのシバタさん

9:00am
Departure from Hamamatsu-cho station!
浜松町駅から出発!

9:10am
Tokyo Tower visit (➡P44)
「東京タワー」を見学

10:05am
Tea time at HAPPO-EN (➡P47)
「八芳園」でお茶の時間

11:40pm
Yakiniku BBQ lunch at Chinzan-so
「椿山荘」でバーベキュー

1:50pm
Imperial Palace visit (➡P42)
「皇居」前で記念撮影

3:00pm
Sumidagawa River cruise
「隅田川クルーズ」

3:50pm
Sensoji Temple & Nakamise (➡P12)
「浅草寺」と「仲見世」

Dynamic Tokyo Tour
Ⓣ03-3435-6081 (Reservation accepted for 9am-6:30pm)
Ⓞ9am-5:10pm daily Ⓕ¥12000

WORD BOOK

単語帳

Let's start from hello!

「こんにちは」からはじめよう！

Greetings
あいさつ
Aisatsu

Good morning グッドモーニング おはよう Ohayō	**Good evening** グッド イヴニング こんばんは kon'banwa	**Good bye** グッド バイ さようなら sayōnara	**Thank you.** サンキュー ありがとう Arigatō
Good night グッド ナイト おやすみなさい oyasumi nasai	**I am sorry.** アイ アム ソーリー ごめんなさい gomen nasai	**See you.** スィー ユー じゃあね jaa ne	**Yes** イエス はい hai
No ノー いいえ iie	**I'm from U.K.** アイム フロム ユーケー 私はイギリス出身です watashi wa igirisu shusshin desu	**Please call me Nick.** プリーズ コール ミー ニック ニック と呼んでください nikku to yonde kudasai	**I understand.** アイ アンダースタンド わかりました wakari mashita
I must be going. アイ マスト ビー ゴーイング 失礼します shitsurei shimasu	**You're welcome.** ユーアー ウェルカム どういたしまして dō itashimashite	**No, thank you.** ノー サンキュー 結構です kekkō desu	**What do you do?** ホァット ドゥ ユー ドゥ 仕事は何ですか? shigoto wa nan desuka?
I'm a student. アイム ア スチューデント 学生です gakusei desu	**I'm an office worker.** アイム アン オフィス ワーカー 会社員です kaishain desu	**What are your hobbies?** ホァット アー ユア ホビィズ 趣味は何ですか? shumi wa nan desuka?	**I like soccer.** アイ ライク サッカー サッカーが好きです sakkā ga suki desu

When greeting, Japanese bow many times to each other.
日本人は挨拶をするときにお互いに何度もおじぎをする

Conversation

日常会話

Nichijo kaiwa

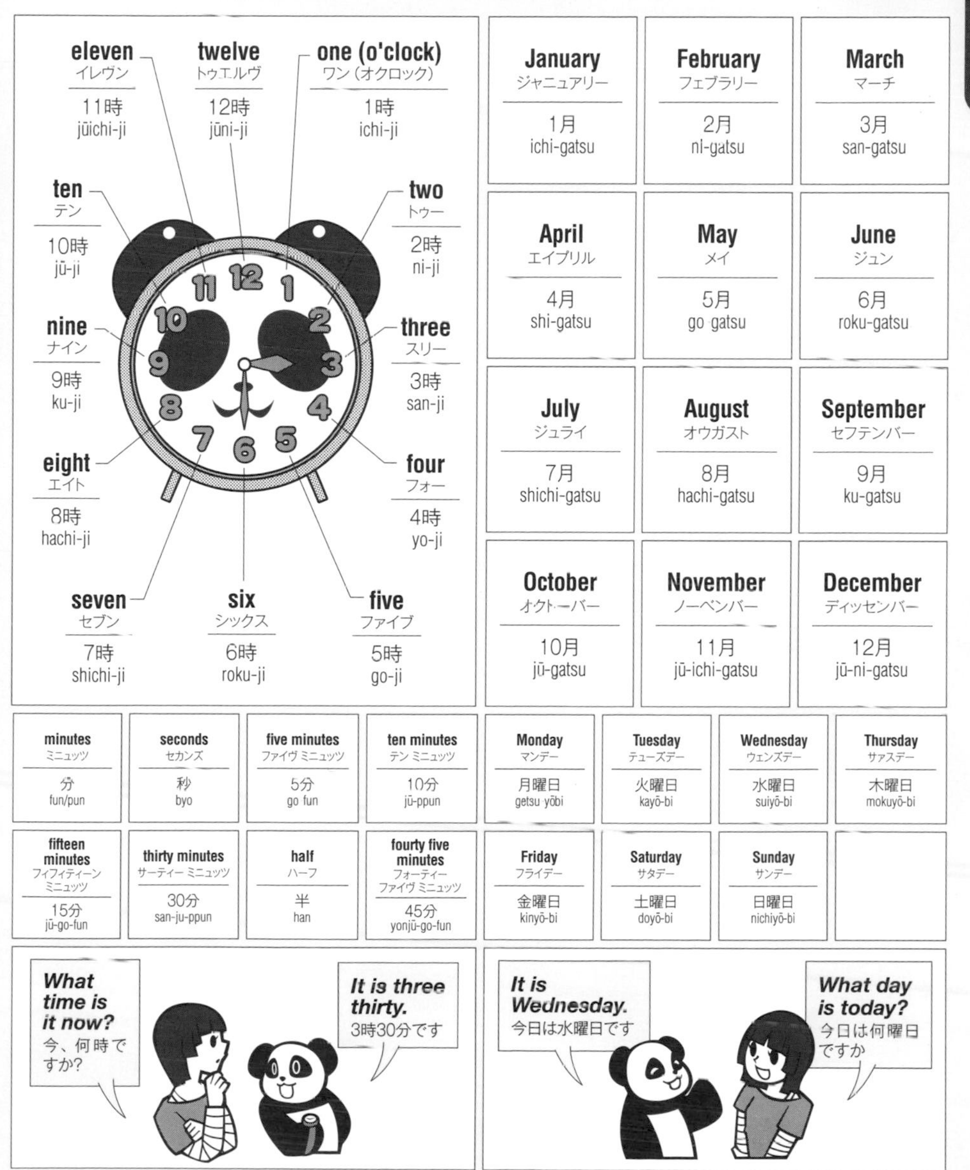

There are many stores that never close in Tokyo, most convenience stores are open 24 hours a day
東京にはコンビニなど24時間営業の店が多い

What's the date? ホァッツ ダ デイト

今日は何月何日ですか kyōwa nangatsu nan'nichi desuka?

Today is May 10th. トゥデイ イズ メイ テンス

今日は5月10日です kyō wa go-gatsu tō-ka desu.

When is your birthday? ホェン イズ ユア バースデー

あなたの誕生日はいつですか anata no tanjōbi wa itsu desuka?

My birthday is January 20th.
マイ バースデー イズ ジャニュアリー トゥエンティース

私の誕生日は1月20日です watashi no tanjōbi wa ichi gatsu hatsuka desu.

morning
モーニング
朝
asa

during the morning
デュアリング ダ モーニング
午前中
gozen chū

noon
ヌーン
正午
shōgo

afternoon
アフタヌーン
午後
gogo

late afternoon
レイト アフタヌーン
夕方
yūgata

evening
イヴニング
夜
yoru

today
トゥデイ
今日
kyō

yesterday
イェスタデー
昨日
kinō

entrance ceremony
エントランス セレモニー
入学式
nyūgaku-shiki

graduation ceremony
グラデュエーション セレモニー
卒業式
sotsugyō-shiki

wedding anniversary
ウェディング アニバーサリー
結婚記念日
kekkon-kinenbi

funeral
フューネラル
お葬式
osōshiki

holiday ホリデー
休日 kyūjitsu

national holiday ナショナル ホリデー
祝祭日 shukusaijitsu

weekend ウィークエンド
週末 shūmatsu

this week ディス ウィーク
今週 konshū

last week ラスト ウィーク
先週 senshū

next week ネクスト ウィーク
来週 raishū

summer break サマー ブレイク
夏休み natsu-yasumi

golden week ゴールデン ウィーク
ゴールデンウィーク gōruden-uīku

aniversary アニヴァーサリー
記念日 kinenbi

ceremony for new members of a company
セレモニー フォー ニュー メンバーズ オブ ア カンパニー
入社式 nyusha-shiki

Those turning 20 (considered the age of adulthood in Japan) are celebrated in a ceremony on the second Monday of January.
1月第2月曜日には満20歳になった人を祝う成人式が行われる

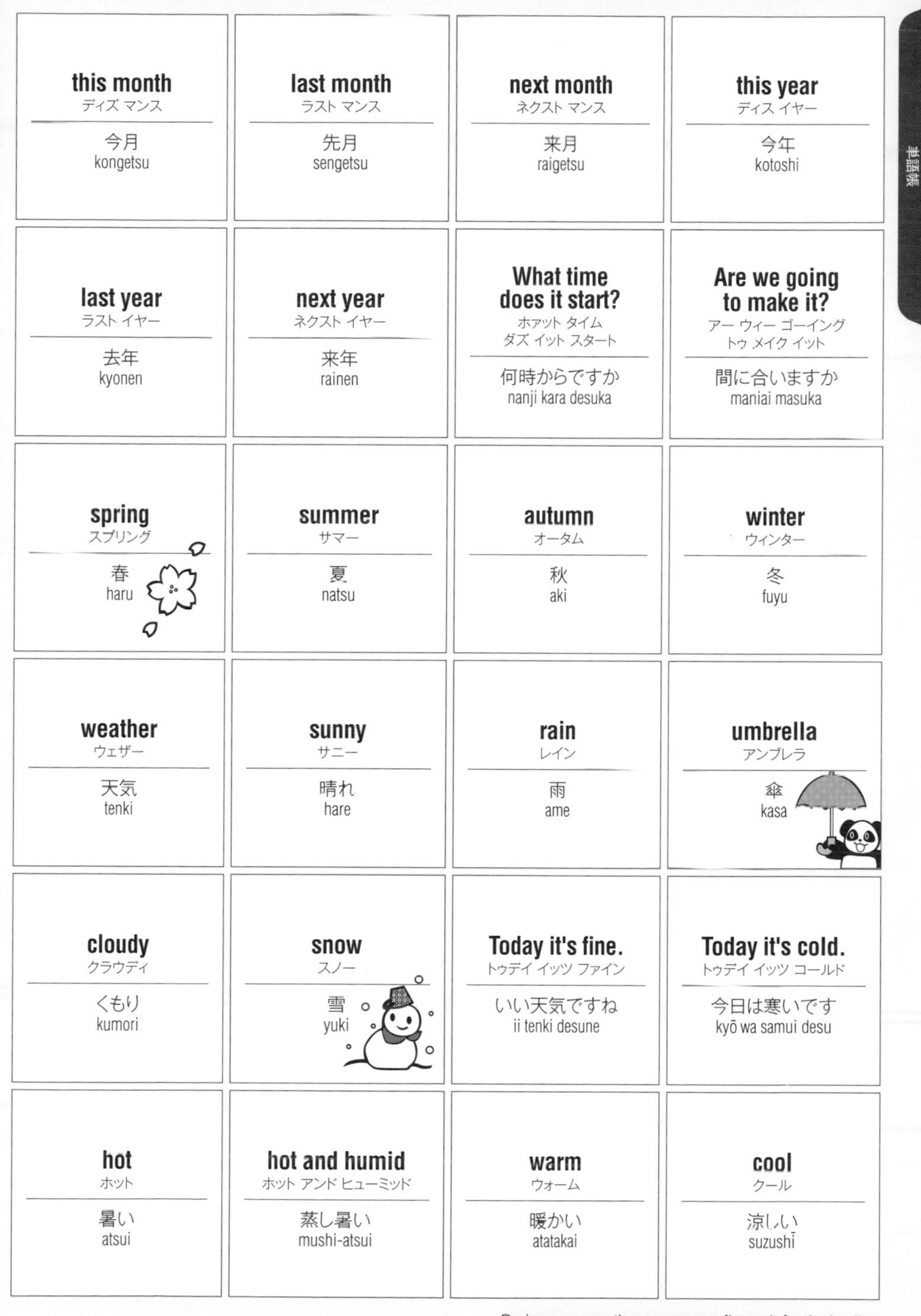

English	Katakana	Japanese	Romaji
this month	ディズ マンス	今月	kongetsu
last month	ラスト マンス	先月	sengetsu
next month	ネクスト マンス	来月	raigetsu
this year	ディス イヤー	今年	kotoshi
last year	ラスト イヤー	去年	kyonen
next year	ネクスト イヤー	来年	rainen
What time does it start?	ホアット タイム ダズ イット スタート	何時からですか	nanji kara desuka
Are we going to make it?	アー ウィー ゴーイング トゥ メイク イット	間に合いますか	maniai masuka
spring	スプリング	春	haru
summer	サマー	夏	natsu
autumn	オータム	秋	aki
winter	ウィンター	冬	fuyu
weather	ウェザー	天気	tenki
sunny	サニー	晴れ	hare
rain	レイン	雨	ame
umbrella	アンブレラ	傘	kasa
cloudy	クラウディ	くもり	kumori
snow	スノー	雪	yuki
Today it's fine.	トゥデイ イッツ ファイン	いい天気ですね	ii tenki desune
Today it's cold.	トゥデイ イッツ コールド	今日は寒いです	kyō wa samui desu
hot	ホット	暑い	atsui
hot and humid	ホット アンド ヒューミッド	蒸し暑い	mushi-atsui
warm	ウォーム	暖かい	atatakai
cool	クール	涼しい	suzushī

During summer, there are many firework festivals all over Japan.
夏には日本全国で花火大会が行われる

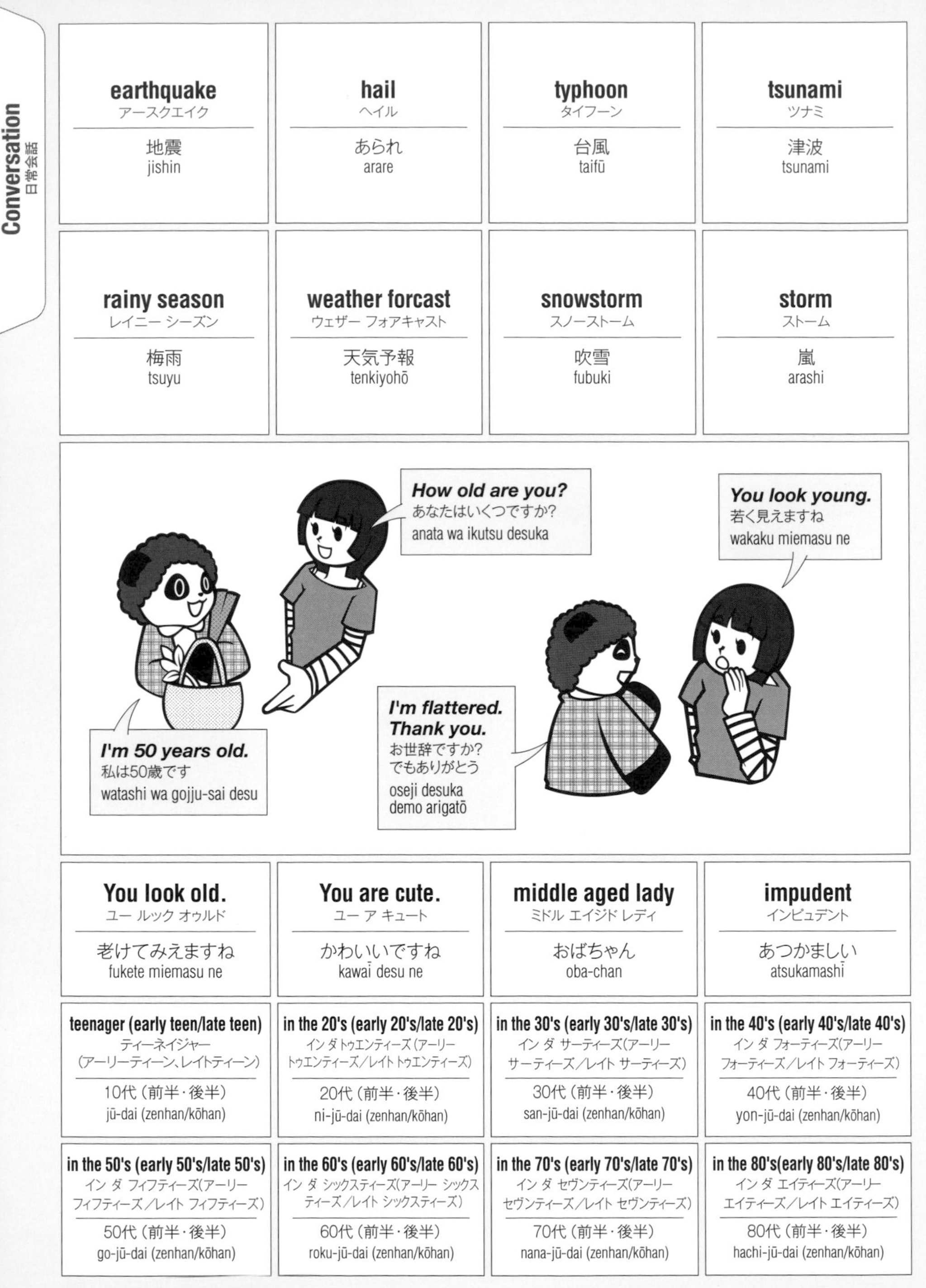

earthquake アースクエイク 地震 jishin	hail ヘイル あられ arare	typhoon タイフーン 台風 taifū	tsunami ツナミ 津波 tsunami
rainy season レイニー シーズン 梅雨 tsuyu	weather forcast ウェザー フォアキャスト 天気予報 tenkiyohō	snowstorm スノーストーム 吹雪 fubuki	storm ストーム 嵐 arashi

You look old. ユー ルック オウルド 老けてみえますね fukete miemasu ne	You are cute. ユー ア キュート かわいいですね kawaī desu ne	middle aged lady ミドル エイジド レディ おばちゃん oba-chan	impudent インピュデント あつかましい atsukamashī
teenager (early teen/late teen) ティーネイジャー (アーリーティーン、レイトティーン) 10代 (前半・後半) jū-dai (zenhan/kōhan)	in the 20's (early 20's/late 20's) インダトゥエンティーズ (アーリー トゥエンティーズ/レイト トゥエンティーズ) 20代 (前半・後半) ni-jū-dai (zenhan/kōhan)	in the 30's (early 30's/late 30's) イン ダ サーティーズ(アーリー サーティーズ/レイト サーティーズ) 30代 (前半・後半) san-jū-dai (zenhan/kōhan)	in the 40's (early 40's/late 40's) イン ダ フォーティーズ(アーリー フォーティーズ/レイト フォーティーズ) 40代 (前半・後半) yon-jū-dai (zenhan/kōhan)
in the 50's (early 50's/late 50's) イン ダ フィフティーズ(アーリー フィフティーズ/レイト フィフティーズ) 50代 (前半・後半) go-jū-dai (zenhan/kōhan)	in the 60's (early 60's/late 60's) イン ダ シックスティーズ(アーリー シックスティーズ/レイト シックスティーズ) 60代 (前半・後半) roku-jū-dai (zenhan/kōhan)	in the 70's (early 70's/late 70's) イン ダ セヴンティーズ(アーリー セヴンティーズ/レイト セヴンティーズ) 70代 (前半・後半) nana-jū-dai (zenhan/kōhan)	in the 80's(early 80's/late 80's) イン ダ エイティーズ(アーリー エイティーズ/レイト エイティーズ) 80代 (前半・後半) hachi-jū-dai (zenhan/kōhan)

Tsunami is also Tsunami in English.
津波は英語でもTsunamiとよばれる

children チルドレン 子供 kodomo	young people ヤング ピープル 若者 wakamono	elderly エルダリー お年寄り otoshiyori	man and woman マン エンド ウーマン 男性と女性 dansei to josei
Let's go to Karaoke! レッツ ゴー トゥー カラオケ カラオケに行こうよ karaoke ni ikōyo	May I smoke? メイ アイ スモーク タバコを吸ってもいいですか tabako o sutte mo īdesuka	Please take your shoes off. プリーズ テイク ユア シューズ オフ 靴を脱いでください kutsu o nuide kudasai	Let's decide with paper scissors rock'! レッツ ディサイド ウィズ ペパー シザーズ ロック じゃんけんで決めよう (グー、チョキ、パー) janken de kimeyō (gū,choki pā)
I am going to work overtime today. アイ アム ゴーイング トゥ ワーク オヴァータイム トゥデイ 今日は残業です kyō wa zangyō desu	This is trendy now. ディス イズ トレンディ ナウ これは流行っています kore wa hayatte imasu	right? ライト でしょ? deshō	I see. アイ スィ そうなんだ sōnanda
husband ハズバンド 夫 otto	wife ワイフ 妻 tsuma	parents ペアレンツ 両親 ryōshin	father ファーダー 父 chichi
mother マダー 母 haha	son サン 息子 musuko	daughter ドータァー 娘 musume	big brother ビッグ ブラダー 兄 ani
big sister ビッグ シスター 姉 ane	little brother リトル ブラダー 弟 otōto	little sister リトル シスター 妹 imōto	uncle アンクル 叔父 oji
aunt アウント 叔母 oba	grand father グランド ファーダー 祖父 sofu	grand mother グランド マダー 祖母 sobo	cousin カズン いとこ itoko
pet ペット ペット potto	How many brothers do you have? ハウ メニー ブラダーズ ドゥ ユー ハヴ 兄弟は何人いますか kyōdai wa nan'nin imasuka	Where do you live? ホェア ドゥ ユー リヴ どこに住んでいますか dokoni sunde imasuka	I am single. アイ アム シングル 独身です dokushin desu
What do you want to do? ホアット ドゥ ユー ウォント トゥ ドゥ どうする? dōsuru	You see, ユー スィー あのね anone	That can't be true. ダット キャント ビー トゥルー まさか! masaka	That's right! ダッツ ライト その通り! sonotōri

In Japan, regular apartments are called mansions.
英語で大豪邸を意味する「マンション」は、日本では中高層の集合住宅のことを意味する

Sightseeing
見る
Miru

In Tokyo, people stand on the left side of escalator to let others who are in a rush to walk up the escalator on the right side. In Osaka, people stand on the opposite side, on the right.
東京でエスカレーターは左側に立ち、右側を急ぐ人のために空けるが、大阪ではなぜか逆

Where is the Isetan Department store?
ホェア イズ ダ イセタン デパートメント ストア

伊勢丹デパートはどこですか
Isetan depāto wa doko desuka

I'm looking for a rest room.
アイム ルッキング フォー アレスト ルーム

トイレを探しています
toire o sagashite imasu

I would like to visit Tokyo tower.
アイ ウッド ライク トゥ ヴィジット トーキョー タワー

東京タワーへ行きたいです
tōkyō tawā e ikitai desu

Will you take a picture of us?
ウィル ユー テイク ア ピクチャー オブ アス

写真を撮ってください
shashin o totte kudasai

I would like to see Sensōji.
アイ ウッド ライク トゥ スィ センソージ

浅草寺が見たいです
sensō-ji ga mitai desu

How long does it take?
ハウ ロング ダズ イット テイク

時間はどのくらいかかりますか
jikan wa donokurai kakari masuka

How much does it take?
ハウ マッチ ダズ イット テイク

お金はどのくらいかかりますか
okane wa donokurai kakari masuka

I see
アイ スィ

わかりました
wakarimashita

I am OK.
アイ アム オウケー

大丈夫です
daijōbu desu

beautiful
ビューティフル

きれい
kirei

dirty
ダーティー

汚い
kitanai

not so good
ノット ソー グッド

いまいち
imaichi

quite
クワイト

かなり
kanari

great
グレイト

すごい
sugoi

wonderful
ワンダフル

すばらしい
subarashi

not a big deal
ノット ア ビッグ ディール

たいしたことない
taishitakotonai

interesting
インタレスティング

おもしろい
omoshiroi

unbelievable
アンビリーバブル

信じられない
shinjirarenai

very rare
ヴェリー レア

とても珍しい
totemo mezurashi

I have never seen anything like this before.
アイ ハヴ ネヴァー シーン エーシィング ライク ディス ビフォア

こんなもの初めて見ました
kon'namono hajimete mimashita

"Depa-chika" is the basement floor of department stores and there are many stores selling groceries . They are usually delicious and popular.
「デパ地下」にはスイーツや生鮮食料品が売られている

English	Katakana	Japanese	Romaji
this way	ディス ウェイ	こっち	kocchi
that way	ダット ウェイ	あっち	acchi
over there	オーヴァー デア	そっち	socchi
which	フィッチ	どっち	docchi
I like here.	アイ ライク ヒア	ここが好きです	kokoga suki desu
far	ファー	遠い	tōi
near	ニア	近い	chikai
straight	ストレート	まっすぐ	massugu
train	トレイン	電車	densha
station	ステーション	駅	eki
transit	トランジット	乗り換え	norikae
bullet train	ボレット トレイン	新幹線	shinkansen
limited express train	リミティッド エクスプレス トレイン	特急電車	tokkyu densha
Ginza line, subway	ギンザ ライン サブウェイ	地下鉄銀座線	chikatetsu ginzasen
ticket gate	ティケット ゲイト	改札口	kaisatsuguchi
ticket	ティケット	切符	kippu
ticket machine	ティケット マシーン	切符販売機	kippu hanbaiki
(sexual) pervert	(セクシュアル) パーバート	痴漢	chikan
priority seats	プライオリティ シーツ	優先席	yūsenseki
ads hanging on the train	アズ ハンギング オン ダ トレイン	中吊り広告	nakazurikōkoku
bus stop	バス ストップ	バス停	basutei
taxi	タクシー	タクシー	takushi
intersection	インターセクション	交差点	kōsaten
traffic jam	トラフィック ジャム	渋滞	jūtai

The ads on the train sometimes have photos that are not appropriate for children to look.
電車内の中吊り広告には、子供が見てはいけないような写真までのっていることも

English	カタカナ	日本語	Romaji
telephone number	テレフォン ナンバー	電話番号	denwabangō
address	アドレス	住所	jūsho
time	タイム	時間	jikan
distance	ディスタンス	距離	kyori
right(left)side	ライト（レフト）サイド	右（左）側	migi(hidari)gawa
turn right(left)	ターン ライト（レフト）	右（左）へ曲がる	migi(hidari) e magaru
I love Roppongi.	アイ ラヴ ロッポンギ	六本木が大好きです	roppongi ga daisuki desu
Where do you recommend in Tokyo?	ホェア ドゥ ユー リコメンド イン トーキョー	東京のおすすめスポットはどこですか?	tokyo no osusume supotto wa dokodesuka
Starbucks	スターバックス	スタバ	sutaba
MacDonald's	マクドナルズ	マック	makku (makudo)
print sticker	プリント ステッカー	プリクラ	purikura
souvenir	スーヴェニア	おみやげ	omiyage
express train	エクスプレス トレイン	急行電車	kyūkō densha
rapid service train	ラピッド サービス トレイン	快速電車	kaisoku densha
local train	ローカル トレイン	普通電車	futū densha
corner	コーナー	角	kado
go across	ゴー アクロス	渡る	wataru
pedestorian crossing	ペデストリアン クロッシング	横断歩道	ōdanhodō
overpass	オーヴァーパス	陸橋	rikkyō
signal	シグナル	信号	shingō
post office	ポストオフィス	郵便局	yūbin-kyoku
police box	ポリス ボックス	交番	kōban
street	ストリート	道	michi
highway	ハイウェイ	高速道路	kōsoku-dōro

People call MacDonald's "Makku" in Tokyo and "Makudo" in Osaka for short.
マクドナルドのことを、東京では「マック」というが大阪では「マクド」という

Meals

食べる

Taberu

"I'm on diet..." There are many Japanese on diets. A lot of magazines have special issues on diets!
「ダイエット中なんですが…」日本でもダイエットに励む人が多く、ダイエット特集を組む雑誌も多いが効果のほどはいかに?

Let's go out for a drink. レッツ ゴー アウト フォー ア ドリンク 飲みに行こうよ nomi ni ikōyo	**Please give me a large serving.** プリーズ ギヴ ミー ア ラージ サービング 大盛りでお願いします ōmori de onegai shimasu	**I'm full.** アイム フル おなかがいっぱいです onaka ga ippai desu	**I ate too much.** アイ エイト トウー マッチ 食べ過ぎました tabesugi mashita
Let's have a cup of tea. レッツ ハヴ ア カップ オブ ティ お茶しようよ ocha shiyō yo	**Can I have the bill?** キャン アイ ハヴ ザ ビル? お勘定お願いします okanjō onegai shimasu	**Let's go dutch.** レッツ ゴー ダッチ 割り勘にしましょう warikan ni shimashō	**It's on me.** イッツ オン ミー 私のおごりです watashi no ogori desu
Can you eat nattō? キャン ユー イート ナットー 納豆は食べられますか nattō wa taberaremasuka	**This is awful.** ディス イズ オーフル まずい mazui	**so-so** ソウ ソウ まあまあ māmā	**I can't eat this.** アイ キャント イート ディス これは食べられません kore wa taberaremasen
sweet スイート 甘い amai	**hot** ホット 辛い karai	**salty** ソルティ しょっぱい shoppai	**sour** サワー すっぱい suppai
taste strong / thick テイスト ストロング／ティック 味が濃い（薄い） aji ga koi(usui)	**bitter** ビター 苦い nigai	**I'm thirsty** アイム タースティ のどが渇きました nodoga kawakimashita	**Another bowl, please!** アナザー ボウル プリーズ おかわり! okawari
Cheers! チアーズ 乾杯! kampai	**specialty** スペシャリティ 名物料理 meibutsu-ryōri	**This is extremely delicious.** ディス イズ エクストリムリ デリシャス 激ウマです geki uma desu	**This is very good.** ディス イズ ウェリー グッド 超おいしいです cho oishi desu

In Japan,when a man and a woman go out to eat, they often split the bill unless they are in a special relationship.
日本では男性と女性が食事をしても、恋人ではないかぎり「割り勘」が普通

Japanese food ジャパニーズ フード 日本料理 nihon-ryōri	**Chinese food** チャイニーズ フード 中国料理 chūgoku-ryōri	**Korean food** コリアン フード 韓国料理 kankoku-ryōri	**French food** フレンチ フード フランス料理 furansu-ryōri
home made meals ホーム メイド ミールズ 家庭料理 katei-ryōri	**mother's home cooking** マダーズ ホーム クッキング お袋の味 ofukuro no aji	**lunch box** ランチ ボックス お弁当 obentō	**A cup of hot tea, please.** ア カップ オブ ホット ティー プリーズ あたたかい お茶をください atatakai ocha o kudasai
breakfast ブレックファスト 朝食 chōshoku	**lunch** ランチ 昼食 chūshoku	**dinner** ディナー 夕食 yūshoku	**afternoon snack** アフタヌーン スナック おやつ oyatsu
beef ビーフ 牛肉 gyūniku	**pork** ポーク 豚肉 butaniku	**chicken** チキン 鶏肉 toriniku	**fish** フィッシュ 魚 sakana
vegetable ヴェジタブル 野菜 yasai	**fruit** フルート 果物 kudamono	**milk** ミルク 牛乳 gyūnyū	**beer** ビア ビール bīru
hot sake ホット サケ 熱燗 atsukan	**cold sake** コウルド サケ 冷 hiya	**clear liquor** クリア リカー 焼酎 shōchū	**hang over** ハング オーヴァー 二日酔い futsuka-yoi

At drug stores, they sell many kinds of vitamin drinks for hang overs.
薬局には二日酔い用の栄養ドリンクが多く売られている

fried octopus dumplings フライド オクトパス ダンプリングス たこ焼き tako-yaki	**miso soup** ミソ スープ みそしる misoshiru	**Chinese soup noodles** チャイニーズ スープ ヌードルズ ラーメン rāmen	**fried pot-stickers** フライド ポット スティッカーズ 焼き餃子 yaki-gyōza
rice balls ライス ボールズ おにぎり onigiri	**curry rice** カリー ライス カレーライス karē-raisu	**beef bowl** ビーフ ボウル 牛丼 gyū-don	**chicken & egg bowl** チキン アンド エッグ ボウル 親子丼 oyako-don
fish cakes in a pot フィッシュ ケイクス イン ア ポット おでん oden	**grilled chicken on sticks** グリルド チキン オン スティックス 焼き鳥 yaki-tori	**deep fried pork** ディープ フライド ポーク とんかつ ton-katsu	**sweet dumplings** スウィート ダンプリングス まんじゅう manjū
rice flour balls skewered ライス フラワー ボールズ スキュワード 団子 dango	**rice cake in sweet bean soup** ライス ケイク イン スイート ビーン スープ おしるこ oshiruko	**sticky rice cake** スティッキー ライス ケイク もち mochi	**chopstick rest** チョップスティック レスト 箸置き hashi-oki
wet towel ウェット タオル おしぼり oshibori	**Chinese spoon** チャイニーズ スプーン れんげ renge	**scooper** スクーパー おたま otama	**toothpicks** トゥースピックス つまようじ tsumayōji
cup ramen カップ ラーメン カップ麺 kappumen	**omelet fried rice** オムレット フライド ライス オムライス omuraisu	**fried noodles** フライド ヌードルス 焼きそば yakisoba	**hot-plate pizza** ホット プレイト ピッツァ お好み焼き okonomiyaki

"Dumplings rather than flowers" The proverb means people prefer something practical.
「花よりだんご」実質的なもののほうがよいということわざ

Some Japanese coins have hole in the center. Tourists sometimes use them as accessories.
日本には穴の開いているコインがある。紐を通してアクセサリーにする外国人もいるとか?

I'd like to buy chopsticks. アイド ライク トゥ バイ チョップスティックス 箸が買いたいです hashi ga kaitai desu	**Too expensive** トゥ イクスペンシヴ 高いです takai desu	**Please give me a discount.** プリーズ ギヴ ミー ア ディスカウント まけてください makete kudasai	**Can I try it on?** キャン アイ トライ イット オン 試着していいですか shichaku shite īdesuka
What colors do you have? ホアット カラーズ ドゥ ユーハヴ 何色がありますか nani-iro ga arimasuka	**Are there different sizes?** アー デア ディファレント サイズィーズ 他のサイズはありますか hoka no saizu wa arimasuka	**Do you have a bigger(smaller)one?** ドゥ ユー ハヴ ア ビッガー（スモーラー）ワン もっと大きい（小さい）ものはありますか motto ōki(chl-sai) mono wa arimasuka	**Please show me.** プリーズ ショウ ミー 見せてください misete kudasai
Please wrap it nicely. プリーズ ラップ イット ナイスリー キレイに包んでください kirei ni tsutsunde kudasai	**This is fragile.** ディス イズ フラジール これはコワレモノです kore wa kowaremono desu	**I would like to send this.** アイ ウッド ライク トゥ センド ディス 送りたいです okuritai desu	**I'm just looking.** アイム ジャスト ルッキング 見ているだけです miteiru dake desu
Which one is popular? フィッチ ワン イズ ポピュラー どれが人気ですか dorega ninki desuka	**looks good** ルックス グッド 似合う niau	**doesn't look good** ダズント ルック グッド 似合わない niawanai	**fashionable** ファッショナブル おしゃれ oshare
Poor プア 貧乏 binbō	**rich** リッチ お金持ち okanemochi	**I can't decide which one.** アイ キャント ディサイド フィッチ ワン 迷っています mayotte imasu	**Please exchange.** プリーズ イクスチェンジ 両替してください ryōgae shitekudasai
Can I use my card? キャン アイ ユーズ マイ カード カードは使えますか kādo wa tsukae masuka	**small change** スモール チェンジ 小銭 kozeni	**consumption tax** コンサンプション タックス 消費税 shōhizei	**cash** キャッシュ 現金 genkin

Prices include consumption tax.
消費税込みの料金表示となっているのが普通

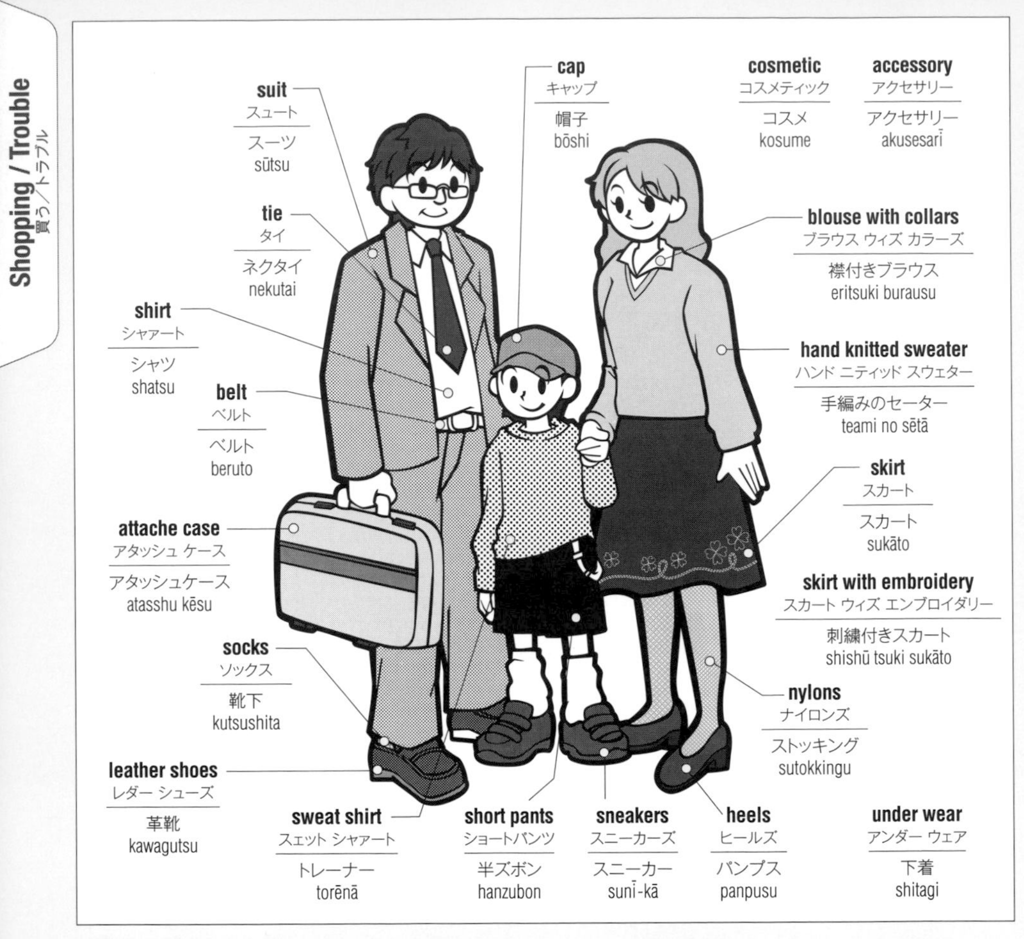

Colors
色

red レッド	赤 aka
pink ピンク	ピンク pinku
orange オレンジ	オレンジ orenji
yellow イエロー	黄色 kīro
green グリーン	緑 midori
yellowish green イエロウィッシュ グリーン	黄緑 kimidori
blue ブルー	青 a'o
indigo インディゴ	藍色 aiiro
grey グレイ	灰色 haiiro
brown ブラウン	茶色 chairo
black ブラック	黒 kuro
white ホワイト	白 shiro
checkered チェッカード	チェック chekku
striped ストライプド	ストライプ sutoraipu
polka dots ボルカ ドッツ	水玉 mizutama

Some people have "Sho-bu-Pants"(win or lose underpants) to wear on a perfect date...
ここぞというときに身に着ける下着を「勝負パンツ」ということも…

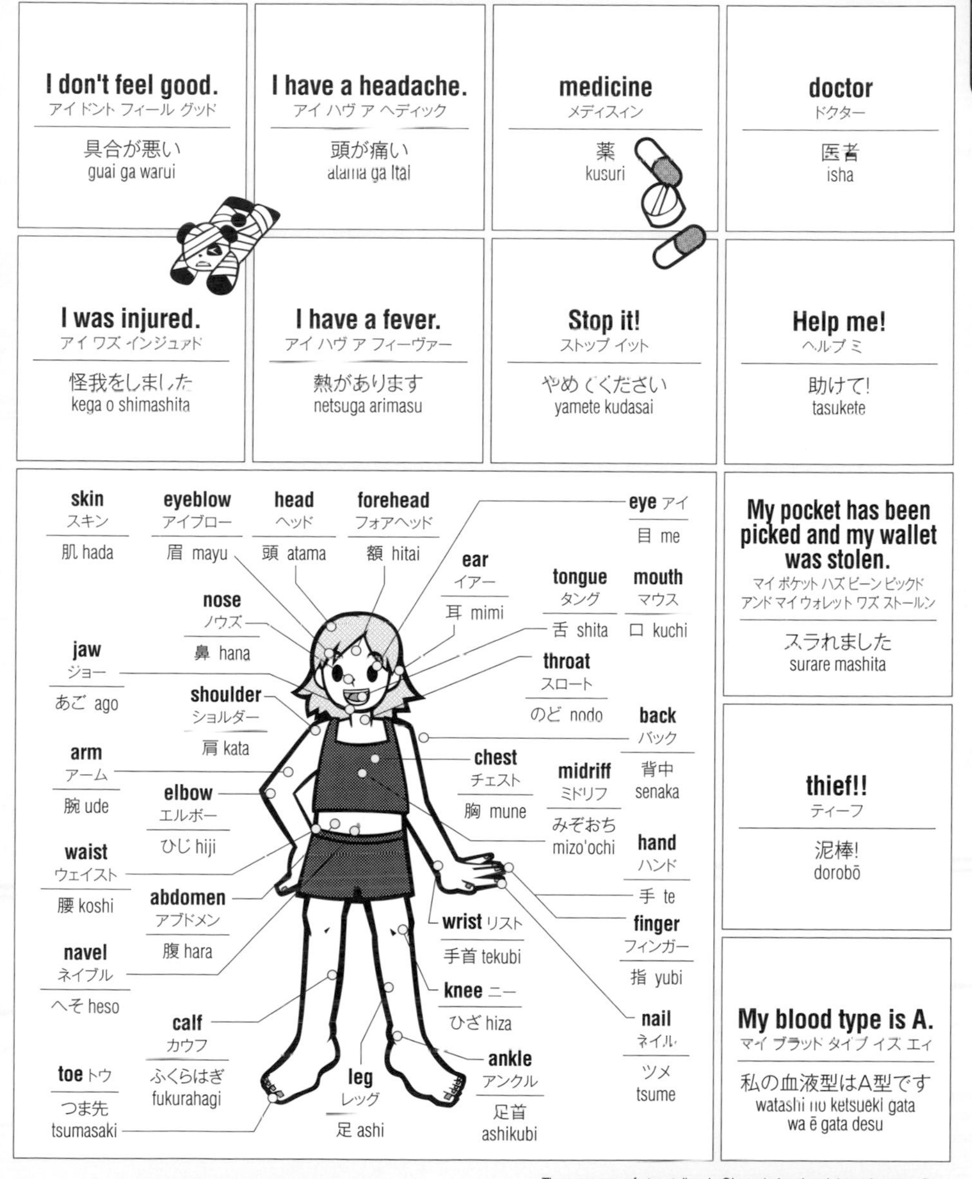

There are many fortunetellers in Ginza during the night and women (in love or looking for love) make lines for them on their way back from work.
銀座では夜になると占い師が路上に店を出し、恋に悩むOLたちの長い列ができる

TOKYO CALENDAR

東京イベントカレンダー

1

New Year's Day

元旦

The Japanese saying "The year's plans are all in New Year's Day" means that whatever you attempt, it is important to plan it first.

「一年の計は元旦にあり」とは、何事もまず初めに計画を立てることが大事であるという意味のことわざ。

Jan~late Feb 1日~2月下旬

Ueno Botan (Peony) Festival

上野ぼたんまつり

Proudly flowering winter peonies. Also held mid-April through to Golden Week.

冬ぼたんが咲き誇る。4月中旬からGWにも開催。

Ueno Toshogu Shrine, Taito-ku

台東区・上野東照宮

6

Fire Department New Year Festival

東京消防出初式

Climb the fire engine ladder, watch the parade, and more.

消防車のはしご乗りやパレードなどが行われる。

In front of Tokyo Big Sight, Koto-ku

江東区・東京ビッグサイト前

3

Setsubun festival

節分祭

Beans are scattered by those whose Chinese animal year it is. This is intended to drive out evil and prevent illness and disaster for the year. This ceremony is held all over the city.

年男・年女による豆まきが行われる。豆まきには邪気を追い払い、一年の無病息災を願う意味合いがある。都内各所で開催。

early Feb~early Mar 上旬~3月上旬

Yushima Tenmangu Ume Plum Festival

湯島天神梅まつり

Around 300 plum trees blossom within the grounds. All sorts of activities occur during this time, principally on weekends.

境内約300本の梅が咲く。期間中の土・日曜を中心に各種行事が開催。

Yushima Tenmangu, Bunkyo-ku

文京区・湯島天神

late Feb 下旬

Edo-Nagashibina Festival

江戸流しびな

Dolls are released down the Sumidagawa River in order to prevent illness and disaster for children.

子供の無病息災を願って隅田川におひな様を流す。

mid-Mar~early Apr 中旬~4月上旬

Akihabara Electric Town Festival

秋葉原電気街まつり

Various events and chances to win shopping coupons, etc. Also scheduled for winter and summer.

各種イベントや買い物券などが当たる抽選など。夏と冬にも開催予定。

Akihabara area, Taito-ku

台東区・秋葉原周辺

late Mar~early Apr 下旬~4月上旬

Ueno Cherry Blossom Festival

うえの桜まつり

Around 1200 blossoming cherry trees. Bonbori paper lanterns create an otherworldly effect at night.

約1200本の桜が咲く。夜はぼんぼりに灯がともり幻想的。

Ueno Onshi (imperial) Park, Taito-ku

台東区・上野恩賜公園

27-30

Tokyo International Anime Fair

東京国際アニメフェア

The world's largest festival celebrating anime. Anime screenings and show events are also held.

世界最大級のアニメの祭典。上映会やショーなどのイベントを開催。

Tokyo Big Sight, Minato-ku

港区・東京ビッグサイト

1 January 1月

2 February 2月

3 March 3月

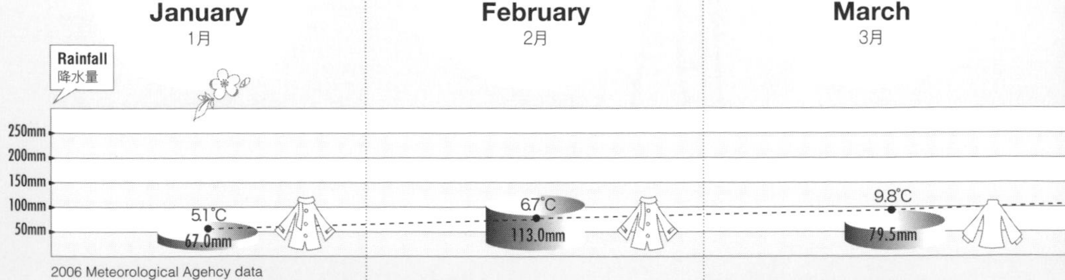

2006 Meteorological Agehcy data

Please note that the schedule of the event and the festival might be changed.
イベント・祭は日程が変更されることもあるので注意して下さい

Apr 5~May 6 5日~5月6日

Bunkyo Azalea Festival
文京つつじまつり

3000 azaleas of around different 50 species blossom within the grounds. Various activities also occur.
境内のつつじ苑に約50種3000株のつつじが咲く。各種行事も開催。

Nedujinja Shrine, Bunkyo-ku
文京区・根津神社

late Mar~mid Apr 3月下旬~4月中旬

Chidorigafuchi greenway
千鳥が淵緑道

Rent a boat and float down the river: it's one of Tokyo's best spots for viewing cherry blossoms.
貸しボートから水面に垂れ下がる桜を見られる都内有数の花見スポット。

mid-May 中旬

Kanda Festival
神田祭

One of the 3 great Edo festivals. The Kanda Festival shinkosai event is held on odd-numbered years.

江戸三大祭のひとつ。本祭の「神幸祭」は奇数年に実施。

Kanda Myoujin, Chiyoda-ku
千代田区・神田明神

mid-May 中旬

Sanja Matsuri (Festival)
三社祭

Most years, this festival sees over a million participants. It heralds the start of summer for the downtown area.
例年100万人を超す人手がある、下町に初夏を告げる祭。

Asakusa Shrine, Taito-ku
台東区・浅草神社

mid -May~late May 中旬~下旬

Tokyo Port Festival
東京みなと祭

Event commemorating the opening of Tokyo port. Cruises and sailboat tours available.
東京港の開港記念イベント。帆船の一般公開やクルーズを実施

early Junr 上旬

Tsukiji Lion Festival
つきじ獅子祭

The festival is very lively, with a female ohaguro black teeth giant lion and shrine parade, street stalls, and more.
雌の大獅子「お歯黒獅子」や御輿渡御、露店などで賑わう。

Namiyoke Inari Jinja, Chuo-ku
中央区・波除稲荷神社

7-17

Sanno Festival
山王まつり

Largest of the 3 great Edo festivals. The shinkosai main event, with a line of around 500 people wearing ancient dynastic costumes, is held on odd-numbered years.
江戸三大祭の筆頭。王朝装束の約500人の行列が目玉の「神幸祭」は偶数年の開催。

Sanno Hie Jinja, Chiyoda-ku
千代田区・山王日枝神社

late Junr 下旬

1000-day shrine visit / Hozuki lantern plant fair
千日詣り・ほおづき縁日

It is said that visiting will bring 1000 days worth of good fortune. The city of Hozuki is also full of charm.
参拝すると千日分のご利益があるといわれる。ほおづき市も風情たっぷり。

Atago Shrine, Minato-ku
港区・愛宕神社

4 April 4月

5 May 5月

6 June 6月

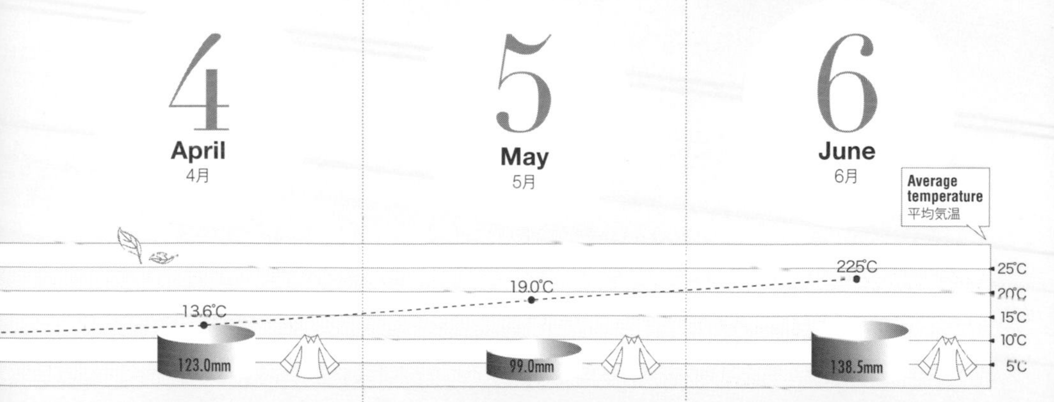

9-10

46000-day shrine visit / Hozuki lantern plant fair

四万六千日・ほおづき市

It is said that visiting will bring 46,000 days worth of good fortune. The Hozuki fair with chiming wind bells is also worth a visit.

参拝すると四万六千日分のご利益があるという。風鈴の音が響くほおづき市も。

Sensoji Temple, Taito-ku

台東区・浅草寺

13-16

Mitama (soul) Festival

みたままつり

Around 30,000 lanterns, donated from around the nation, light up the main approach to the shrine. Around 300,000 people attend the festival each year.

全国から奉納された約3万灯もの提灯が参道を照らす。毎年約30万人もの人出がある。

Yasukuni Shrine, Chiyoda-ku

千代田区・靖国神社

late Junr 下旬

Sumidagawa Fireworks Festival

隅田川花火大会

Around 20,000 releases of fireworks into the sky, with one million or so people attending each year.

約2万発の花火が打ち上げられ、毎年約100万人が訪れる。

7

July

7月

30

Asakusa Samba Carnival

浅草サンバカーニバル

Samba teams gather from all over Japan, heralding the end of the Asakusa summer.

全国からサンバチームが集まる、浅草の夏の終わりを告げる風物詩。

late Aug 下旬

Azabu-Juban Noryo (evening cool) Festival

麻布十番納涼まつり

Many events, such as international bazaar, traditional obon dancing, variety acts, and more

国際バザールや盆踊り、寄席など充実の内容。

Azabu-Juban shopping mall, Minato-ku

港区・麻布十番商店街

late Aug 下旬

Harajuku Omotesando Genki Matsuri Super Yosakoi

表参道元氣祭スーパーよさこい

Around 100 teams from all over Japan participate in one of Tokyo's leading yosakoi dance festivals

全国から約100チームが参加する東京屈指のよさこい祭り。

Omotesando etc., Minato-ku

港区・表参道ほか

August

8月

11-21

Daradara (doodling) Festival

だらだら祭

Considered a festival, it actually runs over 11 days. A ginger fair is also built inside the grounds.

名前は祭りが11日間に渡ることから。境内には生姜の市もたつ。

Shiba Daijingu, Minato-ku

港区・芝大神宮

late Sep 下旬

Shinagawa Shukuba (post town) Festival

しながわ宿場まつり

The main feature is an Edo-style costume parade. You will see kago palanquin and rickshaws, as well as lots of street stalls.

江戸風俗行列が目玉。駕籠や人力車も登場し、露店も多数。

Former Shinagawa-shuku post town of Tokaido road, Shinagawa-ku

品川区・旧東海道品川宿

late Sep~early Oct 下旬~上旬

Fukuro Matsuri Festival

ふくろ祭り

Huge yoimikoshi portable shrine parade on the evening of the initial day, as well as dance performances, Tokyo yosakoi dance contest, and more.

初日の宵御輿の大パレードや踊りの祭典、東京よさこいコンテストなど。

Around the west exit of Ikebukuro Station, Toshima-ku

豊島区・池袋駅西口周辺

September

9月

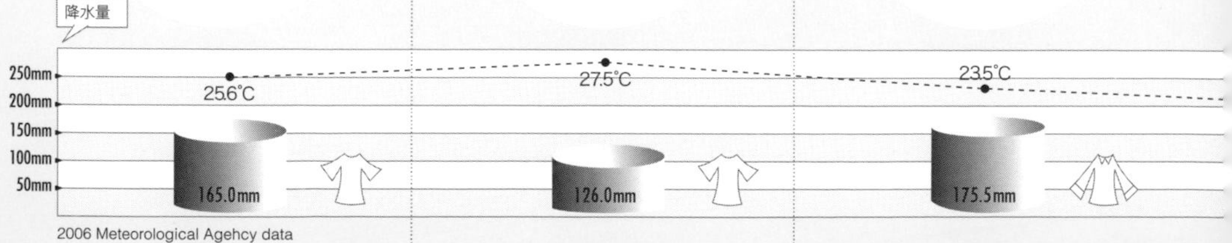

2006 Meteorological Agehcy data

early Oct 上旬

Kappabashi Kitchen Utensil Festival

かっぱ橋道具まつり

Held over a period of one week, including "Kitchen Utensil Day" on October 9th. Sales, a parade, and more.

10月9日の「道具の日」を含め約1週間開催。セールにパレードなども。

Kappabashi Kitchen Utensil Town, Taito-ku
台東区・かっぱ橋道具街

late Oct 下旬

Setagaya Art Town "Sancha de Daidogei (Street performance at Sangenjaya)"

世田谷アートタウン「三茶de大道芸」

Street performances, street stalls, flea market, and heaps more.

大道芸をはじめ、出店やフリーマーケットなど盛りだくさん。

Around Sangenjaya Station, Setagaya-ku
世田谷区・三軒茶屋駅周辺

late Sep~early Nov 下旬~11月上旬

Kanda Furuhon (antiquarian Books) Festival

神田古本まつり

A second-hand book festival held in the book district of Kanda. Many rare books and unusual finds here.

本の街・神田で開催される古本の祭典。珍しい本や掘り出しもの多数。

Kanda Jinbocho antiquarian book district, Chiyoda-ku
千代田区・神田神保町古書店街

The day of the Tori (rooster) 酉の日

Asakusa Tori no Ichi (rooster fair)

浅草酉の市

Well known for its scenery, which the kumade rake shop is built inside the grounds. Ask for good fortune, happiness, and success in business for the coming year.

境内に熊手の市が立つ風景は有名。来る年の開運、綬福、商売繁盛などを願う。

Ootori Sinto Shrine, Taito-ku
台東区・鷲神社

3

Tokyo Historical Festival

東京時代まつり

Featuring a historical parade recreating the history of Asakusa, as well as an Edo-period firefighting show, and more.

境内に熊手の市が立つ風景は有名。浅草の歴史を再現した時代行列や江戸町火消しなどが登場。

Sensoji Temple etc., Taito-ku
台東区・浅草寺ほか

middle Nov~early Des 中旬~12月上旬

Autumn leaves in Kitanomaru Park

北の丸公園の紅葉

Around 300 Japanese maples and 100 gingko trees provide some of Tokyo's most glorious autumnal foliage.

もみじ300本、イチョウ100本などが色づく都内屈指の紅葉。

Kitanomaru Park, Chiyoda-ku
千代田区・北の丸公園

early Nov~Des 25 11月上旬~12月25日

Roppongi Hills illumination

六本木ヒルズのイルミネーション

Over the Christmas period, Keyakizaka Street, the Mouri Garden, and nearby areas are wrapped in an otherworldly glow.

クリスマス時期には、けやき坂通りや毛利庭園などが幻想的な光に包まれる。

Roppongi Hills, Minato-ku
港区・六本木ヒルズ

15-16

Setagaya Boro-ichi (rag fair)

せたがやボロ市

Antiques, second-hand kimonos, and books are on sale. Also held 15~16th January.

クリスマス時期には、けやき坂通りや古着をはじめ骨董、古本などが売られる。1月15・16日にも実施。

Boro-ichi Street, Setagaya-ku
世田谷区・ボロ市通り

31

Zojoji Countdown

増上寺カウントダウン

At the moment the New Year begins, ecological balloons with paper wishes attached are released into the night sky.

年越しの瞬間に、願い事用紙付きの環境風船を夜空へ放つ。恒例の大晦日行事。

Zojoji, Minato-ku
港区・増上寺

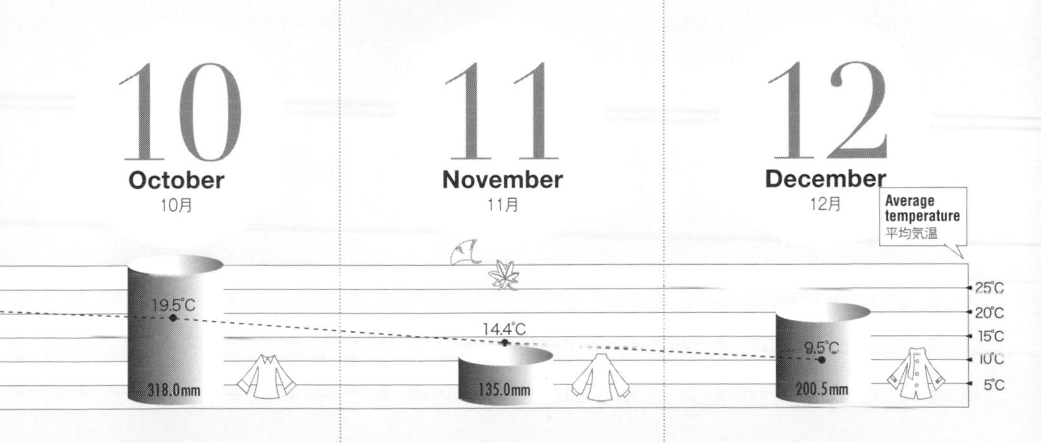

Transportation in Tokyo

東京 交通ガイド

Trains, busses and taxis are the main means of transportation. Trains are the most convenient way to get around if cost and punctuality are your main concerns. JR lines are particularly easy to use even for first-time users, although beware of the morning and evening rush hours when stations and trains become extremely crowded.

主な交通機関は電車、バス、タクシー。料金や時間の正確性を考えると電車が一番便利。特にJRは初心者でも使いやすい。ただし、大混雑する朝夕のラッシュには注意したい。

TRAINS 電車

JR Lines JR線

Stopping at major stations in Tokyo. The Yamanote Line is a circular line fundamental for basic sightseeing. There are also other lines that connect with JR lines, such as the Tobu Railway Line bound for Nikko. Fares start at 130 yen.

東京都の主要駅を通る。観光には環状路線の山手線が基本となる。日光行きの東武鉄道などが乗り入れている。初乗り料金は130円。

JR East Call Center JR東日本テレフォンセンター

☎050-2016-1600 (Japanese)

☎050-2016-1603 (English, Korean, Chinese)

JR Sobu Line

Subway 地下鉄

There are 9 Tokyo Metro and 4 Toei subway lines, each color-coded. These lines finely cover the entire range of the inner metropolitan area. While they offer convenience for traveling from point to point, changing between lines can be complicated.

東京メトロが9路線、都営地下鉄が4路線あり、それぞれの路線が色分けされている。都内全域を細かく網羅しており、どこへ行くにも便利だが乗換えが複雑。

Tokyo Metro

Private Railway Lines 私鉄

These are mainly used for when traveling to the outskirts of Tokyo. Some representative lines are such as that of Keisei Dentetsu — connecting Narita Airport and Ueno, and the Tokyu line bound for Yokohama. There are also others like the Odakyu and Keikyu lines.

主に東京の郊外に行く時に利用する。成田空港と上野を結ぶ京成電鉄や、横浜方面に行く東急が代表的。ほかに小田急線や京急線などがある。

Odakyu Line

Other Railway Lines その他の電車

Tokyo Monorail connecting Haneda Airport and Hamamatsu-cho, Yurikamome connecting Shin-kiba and Ariake, Toden Arakawa Line streetcar system from Waseda to Minowa-bashi, etc.

羽田空港と浜松町を結ぶモノレールや、新木場と有明を結ぶゆりかもめ、早稲田から三ノ輪橋までを走る路面電車の都電などがある。

Tokyo Monorail

Streetcar
都電

Yurikamome Line

How to Ride Trains
電車の乗り方

1 **Find the entrance of the station.**
入口を確認する

2 **Check the train fare to your destination.**
運賃を確認する

3 **Buy the train ticket.**
切符を買う

4 **Go inside through the automatic ticket gate.**
自動改札を通る

5 **Get on the train after checking the destination name.**
行き先をよく見て乗る

6 **In case of riding beyond your destination, adjust the fare.**
乗り越した場合は精算する

7 **Go outside through the automatic ticket gate.**
自動改札を通って出る

8 **Find the station exit.**
出口を探す

Tickets and Fares

チケットについて

Tickets can be purchased at the automatic ticket vending machines near the ticket gate. Child fare is about half of the adult fare. In case you should be confused about the fare for your destination, you can always adjust it (pay the difference) when you arrive at your destination station.

切符は改札付近の自動券売機で購入。子供は大人の約半額。目的駅までの料金がわからないときは、目的駅で乗り越し精算する。

PASMO/SUICA Cards パスモ／スイカ

These are ticket cards that can be topped up for traveling on JR, subway, and private railway lines, as well as busses. There are two types available, both inter-usable. The cards can be purchased at ticket vending machines or at the station counter, and be topped up as needed. A deposit of 500 yen is included when you first pay for the card. With only a tap on the panel installed on ticket gate machines, these cards are make it easy to travel.

一枚でJR、地下鉄、私鉄、バスなどが利用できるチャージ式の切符。2種類あり、相互利用可能。券売機などで購入・チャージできる。預り金（デポジット）500円。改札を出入りするときにパネルにタッチするだけなので、旅行者にも使いやすい。

PASMO Card of Private Lines
私鉄系のPasmo

JR's SUICA Card
JR系のSuica

One-Day Ticket 1日乗車券

There are economic tickets such as Tokyo Free Kippu (Tokyo Free Ticket) allowing non-limited travel on major transportations within the 23 wards, and the One Day Pass for both Tokyo Metro and Toei Subways— allowing non-limited rides on any subway lines in the metropolitan center.

23区内の主要交通機関が乗り降り自由の東京フリーきっぷや、都内の地下鉄乗り降り自由の東京メトロ・都営地下鉄共通一日乗車券などがある。

Tokyo Free Kippu / 1580 yen for adult
東京フリーきっぷ／大人1580円

One Day Pass for both Tokyo Metro and Toei Subways / 1000 yen for adult
東京メトロ都営地下鉄・共通一日乗車券／大人1000円

Obtaining a Convenient Route Map

便利な路線図を入手しよう

Free route maps with color-coded routes are available free of charge from all transportation organizations. Bus

Toei Bus Route Map

Metro Guide

Metro Route Map

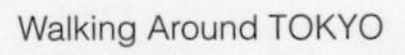

route maps are available at business offices, while subway and JR maps can be obtained at station counters.

各交通機関では、路線ごとに色分けされた路線図を用意しており、無料で配布している。バスは営業所などで、地下鉄は駅の窓口で入手できるが、JRは路線図を用意していない。

BUSES バス

Major busses running inside the metropolitan center require passengers to board at the front and pay the fare by placing the money into the fare box next to the driver before proceeding further inside. With the many bus companies and complicated routes it can be difficult for visitors. However, the Hato Bus can be convenient for sightseeing (see p.80).

都内を運行する主なバスは前から乗車し、運転席横の料金箱に料金を入れて車内へ進む。多くの運行会社があり、路線が複雑なので旅行者の利用は難しいが、はとバス（P80参照）は観光に便利。

Toei Bus
都営バス

Hato Bus
はとバス

Taxis タクシー

There are two types of taxis, company and private, both using the pay-by-the-meter system. When a taxi is vacant the characters '空車', meaning 'vacant', displayed at the front.

法人タクシーと個人タクシーがあり、料金はメーター制。空車の場合はフロントに「空車」と表示されている。

What's 'Eki-Naka'?

「エキナカ」って何？

The term 'Eki-Naka' comes from the words 'eki' (station) and 'naka' (inside), and is used to denote a commercial facility inside a station building where passengers can do shopping and have meals without having to exit the station through the ticket gates. In GranSta of Tokyo Station there are 47 such shops.

改札を出ずに買物や食事ができる駅構内の商業施設。東京駅の「グランスタ」には47の店舗が並ぶ。

GranSta Tokyo

'Eki-Naka' Stations

「エキナカ」のある駅

JR Tokyo Station
JR東京駅

JR Shinagawa Station
JR品川駅

Tokyo Metro Omotesando Station
東京メトロ表参道駅

INFORMATION インフォメーション

Eki-ben

駅弁

Eki-ben is boxed bento lunches sold at railway stations, usually packed with a variety of specialties from the local area. Great while traveling, or even enjoyed at home.

「駅弁」とは鉄道駅で販売されている弁当で、各地の特産などが盛り込まれバラエティ豊か。旅のお供にはもちろん、自宅用にも

You can buy light meals, candies, etc. from the kiosk at each station.
各駅にあるキオスクでも軽食やお菓子などが買える

Available inside Tokyo Station shopping malls and dining area
東京駅構内の売店・食堂エリア

Fukagawa-meshi ¥830
深川めし
The tiny asari clams for which Tokyo is famous are fried and mixed with rice.
東京名物のあさりの炊き込みご飯

The wrapping is decorated with pictures of kabuki actors!
掛紙には歌舞伎の役者絵が!

Kiwametsuki bento ¥3800
極附弁当
An extravagant two-tiered jubako box lunch. Only 30 are created each day.
1日30食限定、重箱2段の豪華版

Gourmet o-nigiri ¥450
こだわりおにぎり
Each one is made by hand. They contain the ever-popular kombu and ume plum.
ひとつひとつ手作り。具は定番の昆布と梅

Tokyo sasazushi
¥1000
東京笹寿司
Sushi formed by pressing rice and filling into a mold.
ご飯と具を型に入れ、押してつくる寿司

Wrapped in bamboo sheathes, these are ideal for traveling.
竹の皮に包まれ旅情満点

You can buy them here.
ここで買える

These eki-bens are on sale inside Tokyo Station, or in the underground malls near the station.
紹介の駅弁は東京駅構内、駅地下街売店などで販売。

NRE stores
Ⓣ0120-658-078 (customer service office)

Eki-benya No.5
Ⓣ0120-658-078 (customer service office)

Daimaru Tokyo store
Ⓣ03-3212-8011

Makunouchi bento ¥1000
幕之内弁当
Grilled fish, omelet, and small steamed items are usual.
焼き魚、卵焼き、煮物などが入る定番

Named makunouchi ("between the show") because they were eaten during intermission at theater shows.
芝居の幕間に食べたことが名前の由来

Sora-ben

空弁

Similar to eki-ben, bento bought at an airport are known as sora-ben. These are usually compact-sized to keep hands clean and lack strong odors; they are intended to be as easy as possible to enjoy inside the aircraft cabin.

駅弁と同様、空港で買える弁当が「空弁」。比較的小型で手が汚れない、においが強くないなど、機内で食べやすい工夫がいろいろ。

Haneda Airport
羽田空港

Shopping area inside Haneda Airport
羽田空港内の
ショッピングエリア

INFORMATION
インフォメーション

Masuno sushi ¥1575
ますの寿司
Traditional sushi with an appealing bright appearance.
見た目にも鮮やかな伝統的なお寿司

Only available from Haneda Airport!
羽田空港限定品!

Okowa sukiyaki bento ¥1500
おこわすきやき弁当
Matsuzaka beef is used for the sukiyaki meat.
すきやきの肉には松阪牛を使用

Sasamaki-okowa musubi rice ball ¥800
笹まきおこわ結び
5 different types of filling. Popular with female customers.
5種類それぞれの具が入る。女性に人気

Koshihikari rice is used for sushi.
すし飯はコシヒカリ使用

Yaki-saba (grilled mackerel) sushi ¥1050
焼鯖すし
Slightly fatty and very juicy, grilled mackerel is popular.
脂ののったジューシーな焼き鯖が人気

Pork cutlet sandwich ¥480
カツサンド
These specially-made sandwich is the volume full marks.
特製トンカツサンドイッチはボリューム満点

You can buy them here.
ここで買える

These sora-ben are sold at stores at Haneda Airport such as Soraben Kobo
紹介の空弁は羽田空港売店、「空弁工房」などで販売。

Haneda Airport Soraben Kobo
Ⓣ03-6428-8775

INDEX
索引

SIGHTSEEING/LEISURE エリア別観光・遊ぶ

EATING&DRINKING 食べる

SHOPPING 買う

STAY 泊まる

TOKYO
The Greatest Travel Tips
英語で歩く東京

2008年4月15日初版印刷
2008年5月1日初版発行

編集人／小松田 淳
発行人／江頭 誠

発行所／ JTBパブリッシング
〒162-8446
東京都新宿区払方町25-5
編集:03-6888-7860
販売:03-6888-7893
広告:03-6888-7831

編集・制作／編集制作本部 国内情報部 第一編集部

編集・取材スタッフ／タンドリーチキン(成田彩子、高木聡子)
宮崎博(方南ぐみ)、四谷工房(鈴木秀行、斎藤京子、野澤正尊)、松尾奈緒美、林みちこ
担当:廣井友一

アートディレクション／三宅尚(BEAM)
デザイン／ BEAM

イラスト／吉野亜弥

撮影／西村光司、宮地工、稲田良平、塚田比呂子、武藤春之介
小杉久美子、横山滋、西崎博哉、村岡栄治
翻訳／株式会社ジーネットワークス、大島希巳江
地図／ジェイマップ、東京地図出版、スタジオDoumo

表紙写真／田中 眞知郎「冨嶽三十六景 33甲州伊澤の暁」(amanaimages)

組版／凸版印刷
印刷／凸版印刷

※本誌に掲載した地図の作成に当たっては、国土地理院長の承認を得て、同院発行の5万分の1地形図、数値地図25000 (空間データ基盤)、数値地図2500 (空間データ基盤) を使用しています。(承認番号平18総使、第80-831号／平18総使、第81-831号／平18総使、第82-831号)
※本誌掲載のデータは2008年2月末日現在のものです。発行後に、料金、営業時間、定休日、メニュー等の営業内容が変更になることや、臨時休業等で利用できない場合があります。また、各種データを含めた掲載内容の正確性には万全を期しておりますが、おでかけの際には電話等で事前に確認・予約されることをお勧めいたします。なお、本書に掲載された内容による損害等は、弊社では補償いたしかねますので、予めご了承くださいますようお願いいたします。
※本誌掲載の入園料などは大人料金を掲載しています。
※原則として消費税込みの料金で掲載していますが、実際の料金と異なる場合がございますので、あらかじめご了承ください
※定休日は、年末年始・お盆休み・ゴールデンウィークを省略しています。
※本誌掲載の利用時間は、特記以外原則として開店 (館) ~閉店 (館) です。オーダーストップや入店 (館) 時間は通常閉店 (館) 時刻の30分~1時間前ですのでご注意ください。
※本誌掲載の宿泊料金は、原則としてシングル・ツインは1室あたりの室料です。1泊2食、1泊朝食、素泊に関しては、1室2名で宿泊した場合の1名料金です。料金は消費税、サービス料込みで掲載しています。季節や人数によって変動しますので、お気をつけください。

All information on this book is based on data as of Feb.29, 2008.
Information about charges, business hours, regular holidays, and menus could be changed. And shops could have an extra holiday.
While every effort is made to ensure the accuracy of all information, you should confirm opening hours, or make a reservation by the telephone before your visit.
Your use of this book is at your own risk. Our company is not liable for any losses or troubles.

084604 711070

TOKYO The Greatest Travel Tips